Teaching Guide

BOOK 3 • LESSONS 61 – 90

Reading Eggs Teaching Guide – Book 3

ISBN: 978-1-76020-086-2

Published by Blake Education Pty Ltd
ABN 50 074 266 023
Locked Bag 2022
Glebe NSW 2037

Ph: (02) 8585 4085
Fax: (02) 8585 4058

Email: info@blake.com.au
Website: www.blake.com.au

Publisher: Katy Pike
Series editor: Sara Leman and Megan Smith
Editors: Sandra Iannella and Stacey Belgre
Designed and typeset by The Modern Art Production Group
Printed by Green Giant Press

Introduction

Reading Eggs

Since the launch of the website in 2008, Reading Eggs has grown to be an integral part of how children learn to read in many schools and homes across Australia and the world. Millions of children have successfully used the program and it's a key learning tool in more than 10 000 schools worldwide. The program has continued to grow and improve with many additional lessons, features, books and teaching resources. The Reading Eggs website now has a vast range of literacy resources including teaching tools, posters, lesson plans, worksheets and more than 2000 e-books, making it the most comprehensive reading program on the web.

Reading Eggs Teaching Guide

The four books in this series cover the 120 Reading Eggs lessons that are the core of the learn-to-read program. Each lesson has now been fully cross-referenced to all other components in the program and to the Australian Curriculum. Whether it's handwriting lessons for the Interactive Whiteboard, apps for student practice on their iPads, whole class alphabet activities, comprehension teaching posters, memorable songs, flashcards or more books to read, you will find a vast range of resources to use in your classroom. Every lesson comes with four student worksheets that focus on a specific skill including phonemic awareness, phonics, sight words, vocabulary, comprehension and handwriting.

Reading Eggs Lessons 61 - 90

This book covers lessons 61 – 90. Each lesson is supported by two pages of teaching notes with learning objectives, curriculum links, classroom activities and a Reading Eggs lesson sequence that links to the four student worksheets. Also included for each lesson are the related Reading Eggs activities, interactives, songs, apps and e-books that can be used to reinforce the content and skills covered in each lesson.

My program

From lesson 11 onwards, the additional *My Program* books appear, with four books for every lesson. These carefully levelled books are a balance of fiction and nonfiction titles, each with their own short comprehension quiz. *My Program* books provide students with the real reading practice they need to improve their reading fluency, vocabulary and comprehension skills. In later lessons, other parts of the program including the Skills Bank spelling lessons, Driving Tests and Storylands appear as part of each student's *My Program* board.

Contents

Reading Eggs Teaching Guide Books 1 to 4 Overview

Lesson	Phonic Letters and Sounds	Phonically Decodable Words	High Frequency Sight Words
Reading Eggs Teaching Guide Book 1 Overview			
1 - the letter m	m		
2 - the letter s	s		
3 - words I and am, and the letter i	a, m, am, i	Sam	I, am
4 - the letter t	t		
5 - the word and sound at	a, t, at	bat, cat, fat, pat, rat, sat, mat, hat	at, a, I, am
6 - the letter b	b	bat	
7 - the letter c	c	cat	
8 - the letter f	f, at	cat, bat, fat, mat, sat	
9 - the word a	a, m, t, at, am	am, Sam, cat, bat, fat, mat	I, a, am
10 - Review	a, b, c, f, i, m, s, t, am, at	am, Sam, at, bat, cat, fat, mat, sat	I, am, at, a
11 - the letter n	n	cat, sat, bat	I
12 - the letter p	p, am	pat	am
13 - the sound ap	a, p, ap	Sam, pats, cat, bat, fat, sat, zap, map, cap, tap, nap, rap, lap, gap	I, am, a
14 - the letter h	h	hat, ham	
15 - the letter r	r	rat, ram, rap	
16 - the sound an	a, n, an	ran, fan, can, van, pan, ant, Sam, bat, cat, rat	I, am, a, an, can, man
17 - the letter z	z	zap	
18 - the letter e, the sound ee	e, ee	bee, tree, see, seed, weed, Zee, three, tee	see
19 - the words see and the	s, ee	Sam, can, see, man, fan, pan, tap, cap, hat, bat, cat, sat, rat, mat, fat, zap, map	see, the, I, can, man, at, am
20 - Review	n, p, h, r, z, e, ap, an, ee	see, can, hat, man, bee, bat, Sam	see, the, can, man, you, I
21 - the letter v	v	van	see, the
22 - and		see, ant, band, rat, hat, sand, hand, land, mat, bee, bat, cat, Sam	and, see, the
23 - the letter d	d	Dan, dad	you
24 - the words in and had		rat, cat, hat, sat, fat, map	in, had, I, can, see, the, a
25 - the letter j	j	jam	see, you, the, can
26 - the sound ad	ad	dad, bad, had, pad, mad, sad, cats, rats, bees, ants	had, I, can, see
27 - the letter o	o	on	
28 - the word is		bee, ant, bad, sad, cap, bat	is, good, a, has, see, the, can, bad, an, I, am
29 - the word on	on	zap, mat, sat, bee, ant	on, the, and, is, a, see, can, you, had, an
30 - the letter q	q	queen	I, am, a, an, at, can, see, the, you, and, in, had, is, on, good, bad
Reading Eggs Posters			
Reading Eggs Teaching Guide Book 2 Overview			
31 - the letter g	g	pig, bag	had, see, the, bad, on, is, good
32 - the letter l	l	lap, lad	
33 - the words he and she		cat, sat, tap, can, jam, van, man, Dan, zap, mat, fat, bee, see	he, she, on, had, the, can, see, is, you, and, in, a, I
34 - the letter k	k		
35 - the words as and has		cat, bat, mat, hat, can, map, rat, man, fan, ham	as, has, is, it, on, a, the, on
36 - the letter y	y	yoyo	had, has, can, is, she, he
37 - the words yes and you		hat, cat, ant, man, van, map, has, and, bat, Dan, can, fat, rat, bad, see, bee	yes, you, has, a, and, it, as, I, am, an, in, he, see, the, can
38 - the letter x	x	box, fox, wax, mix, six	yes, see
39 - the letter w	w	web, win, wig	
40 - Review	am, at, an, ap, ad	van, sad, dam, zap, hat, man, gap, ran, jam, bat, pad, ham, ram, cat, can, see, hid, in, tin, sits, pin, fin	he, she, as, has, yes, you, man, the, can, see, in, and, a
41 - the letter u	u	fun, sun, run	

Reading Eggs Teaching Guide Books 1 to 4 Overview Continued

Lesson	Phonic Letters and Sounds	Phonically Decodable Words	High Frequency Sight Words
42 - the alphabet	Alphabet	cat, mat, rat, ham, map, tap, hat, gap, zap, sat, bat, van, fan, can, man, ran, tan, pan, lap, cap, nap, jam, Sam, ant, fun, sun, fox, box, pin, fin, bee	words, it, the, see, you, yes
43 - the sound id	id	hid, lid, kid, Sid, did, bin, rid, hit, bat	has, a, the, can, see, I, am, yes, it, in, he
44 - the sounds ix and in	ix	six, fix, mix, tin, win, pin, fin, din, bin	in, him, I, can, see, you, yes, a
45 - the sound it	it	hit, sit, bit, fit, spin, lit, pit, wit	it, can, you, on, I, we, and
46 - the sound ig	ig	big, wig, dig, fig, gig, pig, rig	like, said, I, it, my, the, has
47 - the word this		wag, bin, kid, pig, big, wig, fig	this, is, yes, the, it, can, he
48 - the sound ip	ip	lip, zip, pip, rip, dip, hip, nip, sip, tip, wip	little, black, blue, big
49 - the sound il	ill	hill, will, sill, pill, bill, kill, till, mill, dill, fill, gill, jill	
50 - the sound ing	ing	king, ring, sing, wing	bird, two, cannot, has, the, can, this, and
51 - the word go		six	go, by, you, can, see, the
52 - the sound ot	ot	cot, dot, hot, pot, lot, got, jot, rot, not	look, got
53 - the sound og	og	dog, log, fog, cog, bog, hog, jog, rock, sock, shop	of, this, got, lots, the, had, to, go, at, and
54 - the sound op	op	cop, hop, mop, pop, top, shop, stop	play, got, can, the, we, all, in
55 - the sound o	o	lots, dog, hog, log, fog, jog, cog, bog, pop, mop, hop, top, sock, cot, put, dot, hot, not, nod	got, he, lots, of, the, on
56 - the word are		not	are, happy, said, not, this, you, yes, like, no, to
57 - the words his and her		dog	his, her, we, said, like, it, she, this, is, the, he, all
58 - the sound ock	od, ock, ox	fox, cod, rod, nod, god, pod, dock, lock, clock, boxes, sock, rock	
59 - the sound od, y at the end	ox, y at the end	puppy, muddy, bossy, messy, silly, sorry, pod, rod, cod, fox, box, rocks, socks, pot, cot, hot, dot, rot, got	very
60 - Review	ock, ot, og, od, op, ox	clock, dock, rock, sock, lock, pod, rod, cod, dog, cog, jog, hog, log, fog, dot, cot, hot, pot, rot, lot, top, mop, hop, pop, fox, box	
Reading Eggs Posters			
Reading Eggs Teaching Guide Book 3 Overview			
61 - the word me			me, be
62 - the sound up	ut, up	cup, pup, cut, up, but, gut, hut, jut, nut, put	three, green
63 - the sound ug	un, ug	bug, dug, hug, jug, mug, rug, tug, bun, sun, fun, gun, pun, run	
64 - the word to	uck	muck, duck, fluffy, luck, mud, bud	to
65 - the sound uck	uck	fluff, truck, puck, tuck, yuck, stuck	
66 - the word there		leaf, ant, green, duck, mud, sun	there, that, this, hello
67 - the word have		mug, log, cup, green, duck, bug, chin	have
68 - the word they		leg, dog, cat, sun, run	they
69 - the word do		jump, run	do, can, cannot
70 - Review	us	bus, bug, bun, cab, cup, cut, duck, hot, jog, muck, nun, not, pup, rug, run, slug, sun	
71 - the word come		band	come, my, here, goes, day, play
72 - the sound ed	ed, eg, ing	bed, red, leg, peg, beg, egg	baby, open, hello
73 - the sound et	ed, et	bed, fed, wed, red, led, ted, pet, net, jet, vet, wet, hen, ten, pen, leg, egg	
74 - the sound eg	en, et	pet, bet, get, jet, met, set, vet, wet, yet, den, pen, hen, ten, when, men, zen	where
75 - the word where		pen, ten, peg, men, hen, shop	where, when, down, up, go, now
76 - the sound en	eg	leg, beg, keg, peg, peck	
77 - the word who		peck, shell	who, lives, here, into
78 - the word what		wing, tail, log, bed, net, her	what
79 - the sound ell	ell	bell, tell, yell, fell, well, shell, sell, hell	who, what, where
80 - Review		egg, net, bed, red, jet, peg, ten, pen	seven

Lesson	Phonic Letters and Sounds	Phonically Decodable Words	High Frequency Sight Words
81 - the word with	short vowels	pen, pig, leg, log, mug, mop, hat, hug, bed, box	have, with, what, you
82 - the sound ie	ie, ile	pie, tie, lie, smile, crocodile	going, where, want
83 - the sound i-e	ie, ine, ike	lie, line, mine, like, hike	shoe, car, table
84 - the sound ine	ine, ide, ike	dine, pine, fine, spine, shrine	too, off, over, this
85 - the sound sh	sh	shell, shop, sheep, ship, shed	shop, bike
86 - the sound sh	sh	shelley, sheep, shop, shopping	buy, tried, these, new
87 - the sound ie	long i	kite, bite, bike, hike, hide, ride	white, nine, girl, boy
88 - the sound ch	ch	chat, chick, cheese, chin, chips, chest	says, ask, why
89 - the sound th	th	throw, thanks, thin, that, thud, thick, thorn, think	none, two, stayed, home
90 - the sound ch	ch	chimp, chicken, cheese, chilli	these, made, together
Reading Eggs Teaching Guide Book 4 Overview			
91 - the soft c sound	soft c	city, celery, cement, bicycle, park, shark, dark, bark	one, two, three, four, five
92 - the sound ice	ice	mice, rice, dice, slice, line, bike, nine, fine, lime, vine	fly, look, white, fine, nine
93 - the soft g sound	soft g	cage, page, sage, stage, rage	today, park, Saturday
94 - the sound ake	ake	cake, lake, rake, bake, take, snake, shake, make, wake	snake, giraffe, wheel, shark
95 - the sond a-e	long a, ane	cane, mane, lane, plane, cage, ape, game	flew, bowl, brother, everywhere, what, about, another
96 - the sound ace	ace	space, lace, face	clouds, sky, stars, above
97 - the vowels	vowels	life, space	hours, outside, white, purple, yellow, orange
98 - the vowel sounds	long vowel words	make, snake, five, ape	these, out, eight, blue
99 - the sound y	y on the end	itchy, hairy, floppy, rusty, party, creepy	sleep, party, work, easy, flew, plane, high
100 - Review		five, mice, cage	up, down, night, day, in, out, five, nine, eight
101 - the sound oo (short)	oo	cook, book, wool, foot, look, took	dressed, delicious, winner
102 - the sound oo (long)	oo	roof, zoo, noon, moon, cool, spoon, pool, hoop, wood, baboon, cockatoo, coop	moose, cocoon, kangaroo, raccoon, baboon
103 - the sound ole	ole	pole, sole, mole, hole, stole, woke, poke, joke, bone, stone, cone	wombat, ground, kangaroo, mole, phone, poke
104 - the sound o-e	long o, e sounds	rode, code, vote, rose, boat, coat, goat, float, tadpole, flagpole	tangled, seaweed, wavy, bubbly, foam
105 - blends	blends	frog, clam, slam, swam, grub, crab, plug, grab, slug, shell	phone
106 - more blends	blends	crab, clam, frog, fly, green, trunk, lunch, crash, tree	crash, butterfly, hungry
107 - the sound ea	ea	pea, seal, leaf, dream, peach, beach, beast, eat, peace	peace, sitting, scary
108 - the sound u-e	long u words	cube, flute, tune, duke, June, tube	worried, perfect, flute, choose, tongue,
109 - the sound er	er	helper, brother, sister, cleaner, badger, bigger, better, plumber, builder	garden, leaky
110 - adjectives	blends	strong, pretty, dry, crunchy, glossy, flower, ground, cloud, drank, crunchy, squishy	wept, weak, cloud, pretty, adjectives
111 - blends	blends	wanted, trip, crashed, stuck, three	happy, boat, leaf, clock
112 - syllables	syllables	exercise, somewhere, drink, growing, eaten	keeping, drinking, sunlight
113 - end blends	end blends	flamingo, rabbit, duckling, stamp, thump	stinky, wanted, running, wants, keeping
114 - the sound oa	oa	flowers, raincoat, house	picture
115 - the sound /er/	ir	sunlight, seedling, warm, leaf, fingernail	
116 - the sound igh	igh	moonlight, goodnight, sandpaper, icecube, caring	family, forest
117 - nouns	nouns	raincoat, coast, better, bathroom, friends	shirt, goat
118 - the sound or	or	boots, long pants, jumper, coat, cloudy	windy, snow, sunny, rainy, horse
119 - verbs	verbs	remember, imagine, insect, sideways, flap	whistle, squeal, swoop, scuttle, scared
120 - the sound ay	ay	their, apple, spelling, feet, crabs	library, cling, eight, walk

Lesson 61 the words **me** and **be**

Learning objectives

Children will:

- identify the words me and be.
- recognise words for doing actions (verbs).
- read and write using the words me and be and verbs.

Australian Curriculum Content Descriptions

Sound and letter knowledge

ACELA1439 listen to the sounds a student hears in the word, and write letters to represent those sounds; identify and manipulate sounds (phonemes) in spoken words

Creating texts

ACELY1653 follow clear demonstrations of how to construct each letter, learn to construct lower case letters

Expressing and developing ideas

ACELA1435 learn that word order in sentences is important for meaning

ACELA1758 recognise the most common sound made by each letter of the alphabet, including consonants and short vowel sounds; write consonant-vowel-consonant words by writing letters to represent the sounds in the spoken words; know that spoken words are written down by listening to the sounds heard in the word and then writing letters to represent those sounds

Sight words

me, be

Vocabulary words

look, sleep, kick, eat, laugh, climb, read, draw, jump

Extra assistance

For kinaesthetic learners, acting out each verb as you introduce the word will cement the link between meaning and the written word. When you have a list, point at a word and the group has to read the word and do the action.

Classroom activities

Sentence Shuffle

Write and jumble an enlarged version of the sentence: Look at me read. Read it with the children and ask them to work out the correct order. Suggest clues such as capital letters and full stops. Reproduce the sentence on small cards so students can make the sentence themselves and read it.

Mind the Gap!

Write this sentence on the board: Look at me ___.

Ask students to read this sentence by themselves, write it down and fill in the gap with a word of their own. They must then illustrate their sentence.

Reading Eggs Lesson sequence	TEACH Content and skills	PRACTISE Children will:	APPLY
Hear: *Animated Lesson*	Introduce the words *me* and *be*.	identify and read the words *me* and *be* in isolation and in a sentence.	**Worksheet 1** Sight words
Write: *Dot-to-dot, Make a Sentence*	Reinforce correct letter formation. Recognise correct word order for a sentence.	write the word *me*. Choose the correct words to make a sentence.	**Worksheet 2** Read and write
Find: *Word Sort, Golden Goose*	Identify starting and ending sounds. Recognise a given word.	sort words into boxes for start or end sounds. Find the given word in a group.	**Worksheet 3** Vocabulary
Vocabulary: *Blend a Word, The Theme Game, Word Windows, Tiles, Wheel of Words*	Build vocabulary skills: Blend and recognise words. Recognise key vocabulary.	blend sounds to read and make words. Match pictures to words.	**Worksheet 4** Check
Read: *How does it end?, Book*	Read and comprehend a sentence. Read aloud book.	read a beginning and match it to the correct ending. Listen, follow the reading and read along.	**Reading Eggs Story book** Me

Related Reading Eggs Activities, Interactives, Songs and Books

Driving Tests

Test 3

Sight words: me, be

Letters and sounds: at

Spelling Bank

Reading Eggs Puzzle Park

Hidden Words

Song Lines

Do it

Reading Eggs Posters

Reading Eggs Library Books

My Program Books

Critter Card

Me be fish

Teacher Toolkit

Spelling Activities

Grammar Lessons

Reading Eggs Apps

Eggy Sight words

Eggy Snap

me be

Lesson 61 • Worksheet 1

Name

Sight words

1 Trace and write the words.

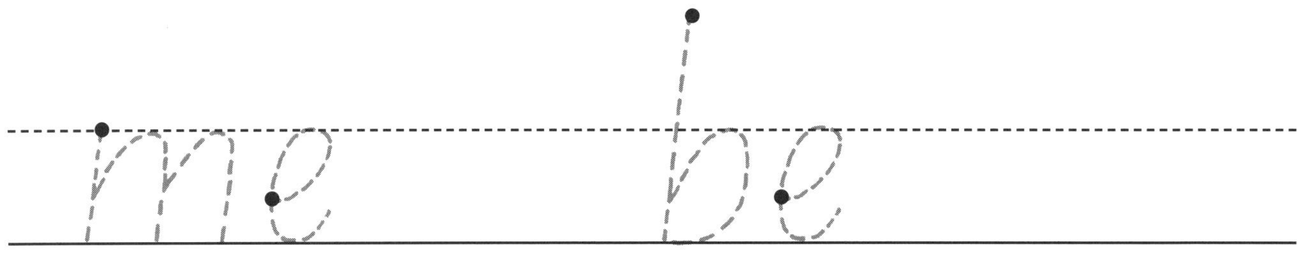

2 Colour the correct word. Cross out the wrong word.

Look at [me] [be] .

Can this [me] [be] a hat?

I can [me] [be] silly.

Look at [me] [be] draw.

3 Guess the word by its shape. Write each word in a box.

me be

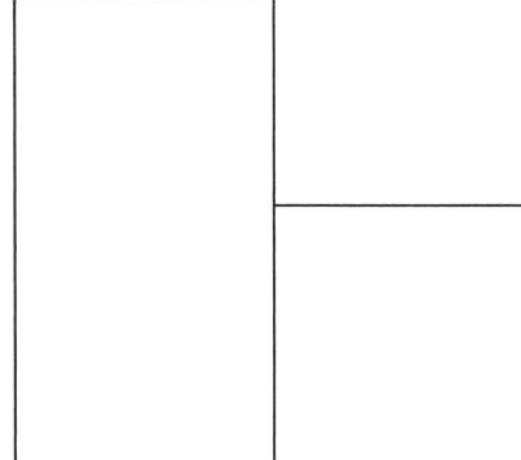

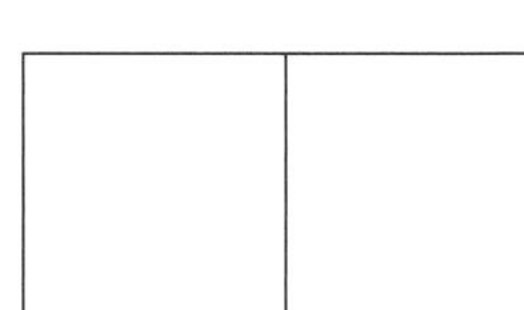

Name

Read and write

me be

Lesson 61 • Worksheet 2

1 Use a word from the box to finish each sentence.

me be Look

Play with ________ !

Can you ________ good?

________ at this hat!

2 Complete the sentence and draw a picture.

Look at ________ run!

Vocabulary

Lesson 61 • Worksheet 3

Name

1 Join each word to a picture.

2 Write your own sentence. Draw a picture.

Name

Check

me be

Lesson 61 • Worksheet 4

1 Complete the sentences with a word from the box.

read draw climb eat sleep

Look at me ____________ .

Look at me ____________ .

Look at me ____________ .

2 Colour the path of **me** words to Me Be Fish.

me	me	be	we	he	be	we
be	me	me	be	we	be	he
we	be	me	me	me	he	we
he	we	be	he	me	me	me

Lesson 62 the sounds **up** and **ut**

Learning objectives

Children will:

- read and write words using ut and up.
- recognise the word up.

Australian Curriculum Content Descriptions

Sound and letter knowledge

ACELA1439 listen to the sounds a student hears in the word, and write letters to represent those sounds; identify and manipulate sounds (phonemes) in spoken words

Expressing and developing ideas

ACELA1434 explore spoken, written and multimodal texts and identify elements for example words and images

ACELA1438 build word families using onset and rime

ACELA1758 recognise the most common sound made by each letter of the alphabet, including consonants and short vowel sounds; know that spoken words are written down by listening to the sounds heard in the word and then writing letters to represent those sounds

Interpreting, analysing and evaluating

ACELY1649 navigate a text correctly, starting at the right place and reading in the right direction, returning to the next line as needed, matching one spoken word to one written word

Word families

up, pup, cup, nut, cut

Vocabulary words

ten, six, three, balloon, red, blue, green

Extra assistance

The short /u/ sound can be difficult for some ESL/ELL students to pronounce. Encourage correct pronunciation in activities and games. For example, use pairs of word cards like *up, cup, pup, cut, but* and so on to play Memory Game. The students only get to keep the cards if they can pronounce the word properly with the short /u/ sound.

Classroom activities

Memory Game

Write the word balloon on the board. Sound it out with the class and discuss the double letters and the word ball within it. Have students trace the word on someone's back or in the air with their finger. Rub out the word and write these words on the board: baloon, ballon, baalloon, balon, balloon. Ask them to identify which is correct, then discuss what is wrong with the other versions.

Reading Eggs Lesson sequence	**TEACH Content and skills**	**PRACTISE Children will:**	**APPLY**
Hear: *Animated Lesson*	Introduce the sounds *up* and *ut* through words and the songs *My new sound is up* and *My new sound is ut.*	sort *up* and *ut* words and match to pictures.	**Worksheet 1** Word families
Write: *Tiles*	Blend and recognise words.	blend sounds to make words.	**Worksheet 2** Initial sounds
Find: *Squirter, 1, 2, 3, 4*	Recognise a given word. Identify the order of a sequence of events.	find the given word in a group. Put pictures in order.	**Worksheet 3** Vocabulary
Vocabulary: *Blend a Word, Catching Frogs, Power Words, Words per Minute, Break it Up*	Build vocabulary skills: Blend and recognise words. Recognise key vocabulary. Identify the number of phonemes in a word.	blend sounds to read words. Match pictures to words. Identify the number of sounds in a word.	**Worksheet 4** Check
Read: *Book Ends, Bubble Popper, Book*	Read sentences using basic vocabulary. Read aloud book.	choose from a list of words to finish the sentence. Read and follow instructions. Listen, follow the reading and read along.	**Reading Eggs Story book** Balloons go up

Classroom activities

Show Me the Sound

Give each student a card with the sound *up* on one side and *ut* on the other side. Say a word and ask students to show the correct sound with their card. Use clear, recognisable words such as cut, cup, hut, pup. Discuss the responses that produce mixed results.

Related Reading Eggs Activities, Interactives, Songs and Books

Driving Tests

Test 1

Content words:

three, six, ten

Spelling Bank

Music Café

Fluffy Duck thinks up

Fluffy Duck thinks ut

Reading Eggs Puzzle Park

Squares

Fingers

Animal Colours

Colour Code

Reading Eggs Library Books

My Program Books

Teacher Toolkit

Spelling Activities

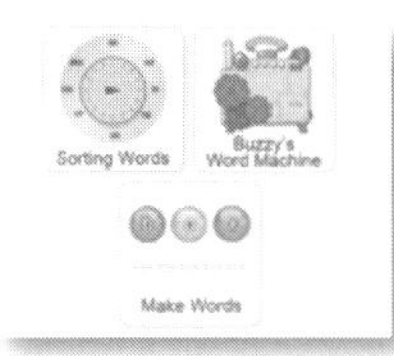

Reading Eggs Apps

Eggy Sight words

Eggy Phonics 1

Reading Eggs Posters

Critter Card

Giddy up

up ut

Lesson 62 • Worksheet 1

Name

Word families

1 Join each word to a picture.

2 Colour the **ut** words red and the **up** words blue.

nutty	less	puppy	silly
zipper	cut	happy	supper
puppy	messy	gutter	but
shut	pup	hut	hiccup

Name

Initial sounds

up ut

Lesson 62 • Worksheet 2

1 Put the letters through the word machines.
What words can you make?

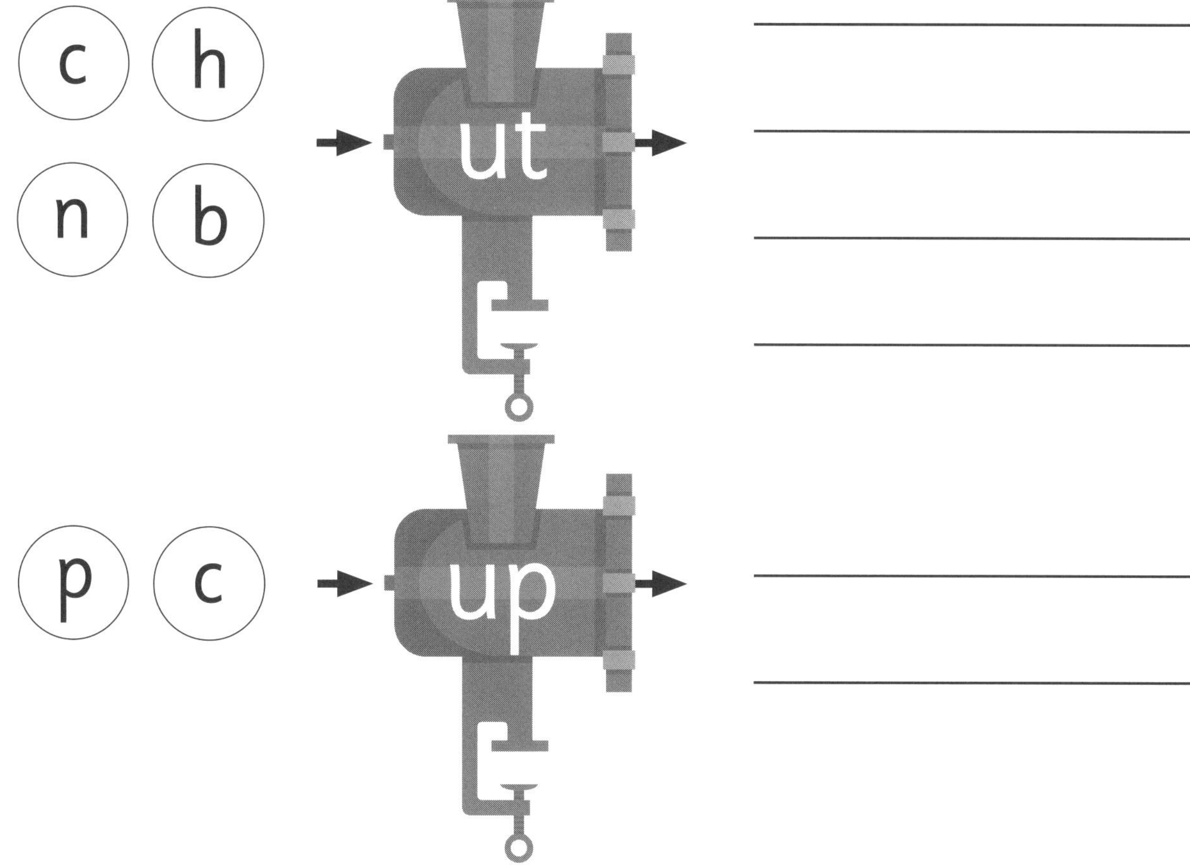

2 Fill in the missing letters.

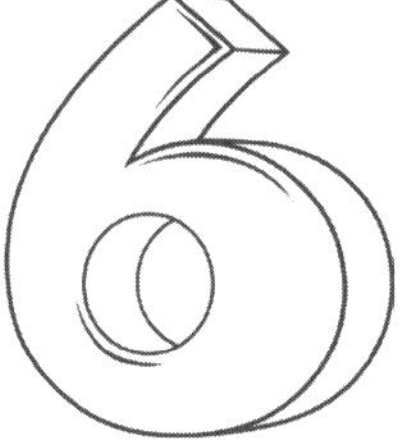

_____ut _____up _____ix _____en

Vocabulary

Name

Lesson 62 • Worksheet 3

Read and follow the instructions.

Draw ten blue balloons.

Draw a red cup.

Draw three nuts.

Draw six green fish.

Name

Check

Lesson 62 • Worksheet 4

1 Use the words in the box to complete the sentences.

three six ten green red blue

Look at the ________ , ________ cups.

Look at the ________ , ________ frogs.

Look at the ________ , ________ socks.

2 Draw a picture to match the sentences.

3 Circle the rhyming words in each row.

nut rat but pet hut cut

hiccup cup tap pup up lip

Lesson 63 the sounds **ug** and **un**

Learning objectives

Children will:

- identify the rimes un and ug.
- read and write words using un and ug.

Australian Curriculum Content Descriptions

Sound and letter knowledge

ACELA1439 listen to the sounds a student hears in the word, and write letters to represent those sounds; identify rhyme and syllables in spoken words; identify and manipulate sounds (phonemes) in spoken words

Expressing and developing ideas

ACELA1435 learn that word order in sentences is important for meaning

ACELA1438 build word families using onset and rime

ACELA1758 recognise the most common sound made by each letter of the alphabet, including consonants and short vowel sounds; write consonant-vowel-consonant words by writing letters to represent the sounds in the spoken words; know that spoken words are written down by listening to the sounds heard in the word and then writing letters to represent those sounds

Word families

nun, sun, bun, run, hug, dug, rug, mug, tug, bug, jug

Vocabulary words

skip

Extra assistance

Many languages do not distinguish between long and short vowel sounds. Give students opportunities to practise distinguishing between the short /u/ sound and the longer /oo/ sounds with pairs of words. Give them two words and ask them which word fits the sentence, for example:

Mud or mood? I jumped in the ____.

Hut or hoot? The owl said ____.

Classroom activities

Mind the Gap!

Write this sentence on the board:

"I can ___," said Sid the kid.

Ask students to read this sentence by themselves, write it down and fill in the gap with a word of their own. Discuss their individual sentences and write a list of possible words on the board.

Throw it Away!

Sit in a circle with a box in the middle. Students each hold two items, pictures or words on cards. They take turns telling what their item, picture or word is. If the object ends with *ug* or *un* they throw it into the box. Discuss the objects with the class.

Reading Eggs Lesson sequence	TEACH Content and skills	PRACTISE Children will:	APPLY
Hear: *Animated Lesson*	Introduce the sounds *un* and *ug* through words and the songs *My new sound is un* and *My new sound is ug.*	sort *un* and *ug* words and match to pictures.	**Worksheet 1** Word families
Write: *Look, Listen and Spell, Ball Game, Tiles, Make a Sentence*	Identify sounds in a word and write the word. Recognise correct word order for a sentence.	sound out a word and select letters to spell it correctly. Choose the correct words to make a sentence.	**Worksheet 2** Read and write
Find: *Word Family, Hairy Heads, Missing Sound*	Identify the correct onset letter to complete the word. Recognise given words.	choose the correct initial letter to make the word. Find the given word in a group.	**Worksheet 3** Vocabulary
Vocabulary: *Word Windows, Rhyming Squares, Word Dominoes, Today's Words*	Build vocabulary skills: Blend and recognise words. Identify rhyming words. Recognise key vocabulary.	blend sounds to read words. Find images of rhyming words. Match pictures to words. Tap on the word being said.	**Worksheet 4** Check
Read: *Book*	Read aloud book.	listen, follow the reading and read along.	**Reading Eggs Story book** We can run

Related Reading Eggs Activities, Interactives, Songs and Books

Driving Tests

Map 3

Lesson 17

Focus sound words:

bug, dug, hug, jug, mug, rug, tug

Challenge: plug, slug

Spelling Bank

Music Café

Sam thinks ug

Jazz thinks un

Reading Eggs Puzzle Park

Hidden Words

Song Lines

What is it?

Do it

Reading Eggs Posters

Reading Eggs Library Books

My Program Books

Critter Card

Tug boat bug

Teacher Toolkit

Spelling Activities

Reading Eggs Apps

Eggy Sight words

Eggy Snap

Eggy Phonics 1

ug un

Lesson 63 • Worksheet 1

Name

Word families

1 Join each word to a picture.

2 Label each picture.

d______ h______ j______ n______

Name

Read and write

Lesson 63 · Worksheet 2

1 Use the words in the box to complete the sentences.

run   in   skip   tip

"I can ________," said Sam.

"I can run and ________," said Jazz.

"You are ________ Sid!" said Jazz.

"I can ________," said Sid.

2 Read the sentence and draw a picture.

Sam the ant tips Sid the kid.

Vocabulary

Name

Lesson 63 • Worksheet 3

1 Colour the **doing** words – the verbs.

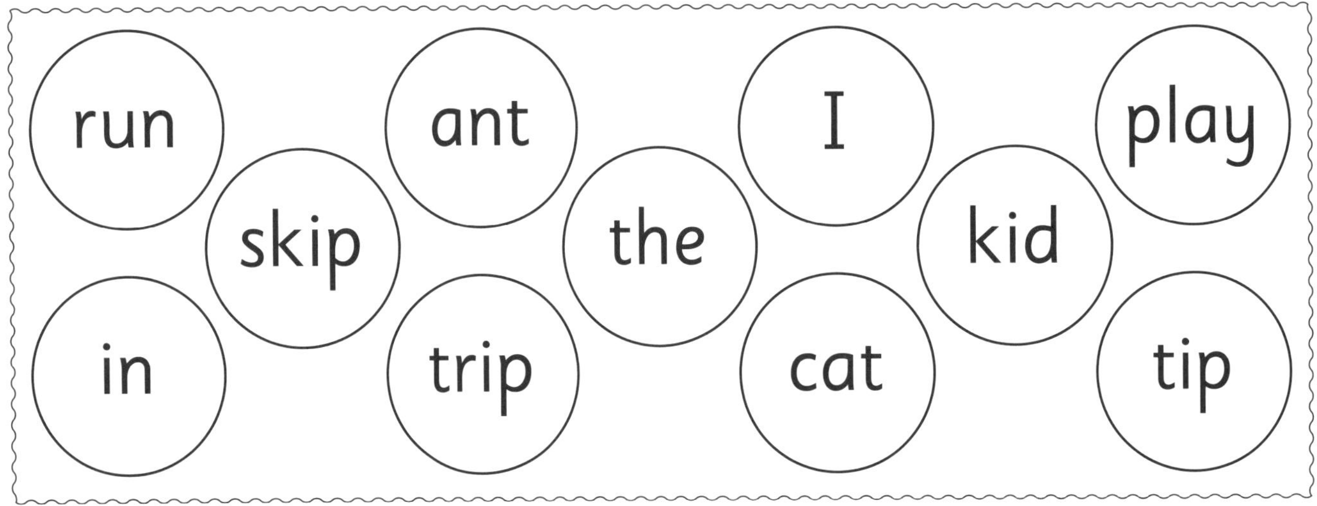

2 Match the jigsaw pieces and label the pictures.

s ips ____________

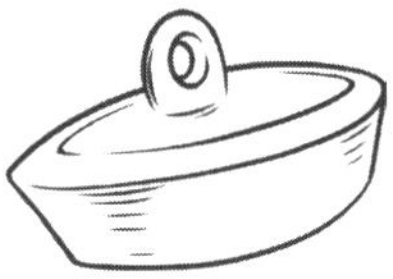

pl ip ____________

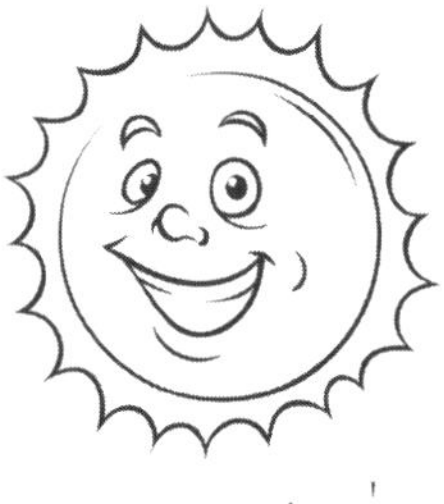

sk ug ____________

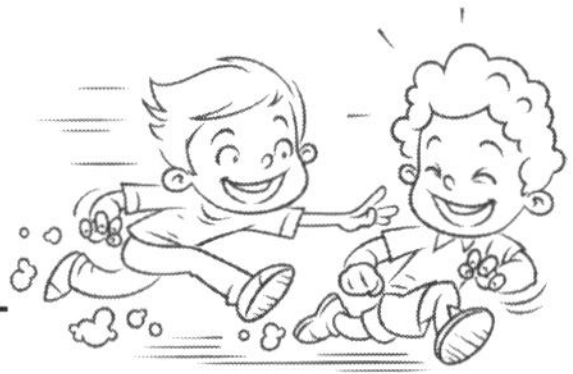

t un ____________

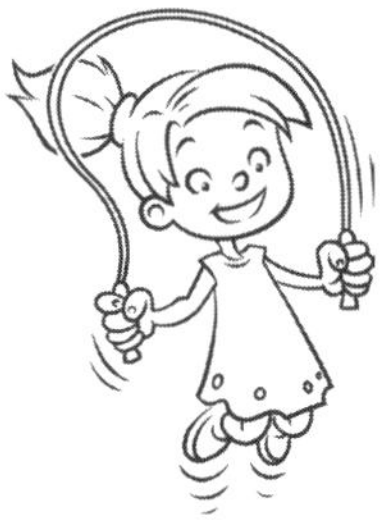

Name

Check

ug un

Lesson 63 • Worksheet 4

1 Write each word.

2 Crack the code!

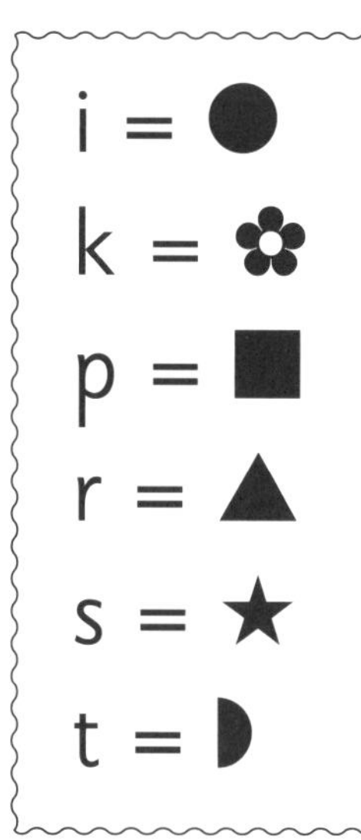

3 Guess the word by its shape. Write each word in a box.

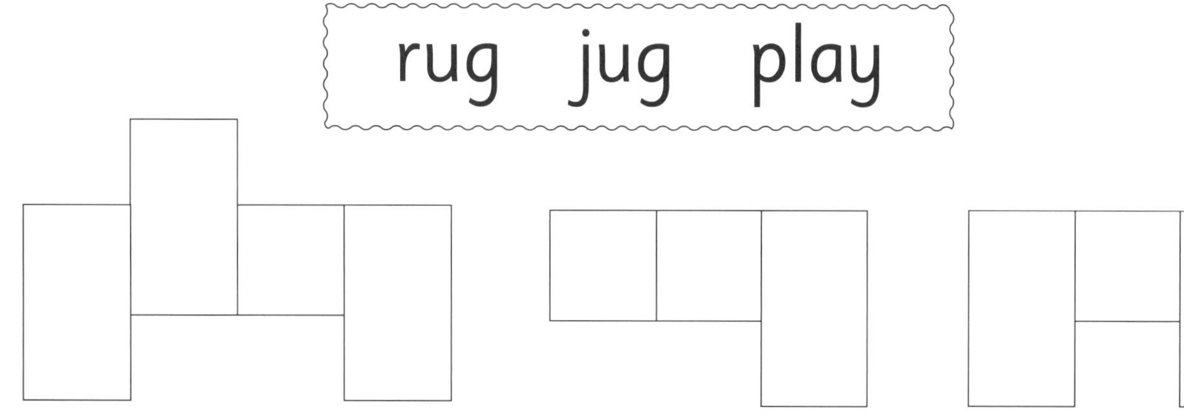

Lesson 64 the word **to**

Learning objectives

Children will:

- identify the word to.
- read and write using to.
- review short u words.

Australian Curriculum Content Descriptions

Sound and letter knowledge

ACELA1439 listen to the sounds a student hears in the word, and write letters to represent those sounds; identify and manipulate sounds (phonemes) in spoken words

Creating texts

ACELY1653 follow clear demonstrations of how to construct each letter, learn to construct lower case letters

Expressing and developing ideas

ACELA1435 learn that word order in sentences is important for meaning

ACELA1758 know that spoken words are written down by listening to the sounds heard in the word and then writing letters to represent those sounds

Interpreting, analysing and evaluating

ACELY1649 navigate a text correctly, starting at the right place and reading in the right direction, returning to the next line as needed, matching one spoken word to one written word

Sight words

to

Vocabulary words

sun, pup, run, mud, fun, dug, up, bug, puppy, muddy, duck, stuck

Extra assistance

Prepositions like *to*, *at*, *on* and *in* are particularly hard to teach and difficult to learn for ESL/ELL students. In some contexts they are interchangeable; in others they are not. They can have multiple uses and meanings. The best way to learn is lots of exposure to their use, so be sure to point out prepositions when reading a text with a class or student, and give them opportunities to choose the correct preposition for a piece of writing.

Classroom activities

Mind the Gap!

Write this sentence on the board: Run ___ the hill.

Write a list of known prepositions next to it: *at, in, on, by, up, to*. Discuss which words could fill the gap correctly.

Now write the sentence: Walk ___ school.

Ask students to read this sentence by themselves, write it down and fill in the gap with a word of their own. Discuss their choices as a group.

Reading Eggs Lesson sequence	TEACH Content and skills	PRACTISE Children will:	APPLY
Hear: *Animated Lesson*	Introduce the word *to*.	identify and read the word *to* in a sentence.	**Worksheet 1** Sight words
Write: *Dot-to-dot, Pick Up Bricks*	Reinforce correct letter formation. Recognise correct word order for a sentence.	write the word *to*. Choose the correct words to make a sentence.	**Worksheet 2** Read and write
Find: *Car and Puddles, Time for 20*	Recognise a given word.	find the given word in a group.	**Worksheet 3** Vocabulary
Vocabulary: *Blend a Word, Find Your Treasure, Power Words, Sound Streamers, Break It Up*	Build vocabulary skills: Blend and recognise words. Recognise key vocabulary. Identify sounds in words. Identify the number of phonemes in a word.	blend sounds to read words. Match pictures to words. Sound out and select letters to make words. Identify the number of sounds in a word.	**Worksheet 4** Check
Read: *How Does it End?, Picture Picker, Book*	Read sentences using basic vocabulary. Read aloud book.	read a beginning and match it to an ending. Read a sentence and match to a picture. Listen, follow the reading and read along.	**Reading Eggs Story book** The muddy puppy

Classroom activities

Run to it!

This is best done in a large room with furniture pushed out of the way, or on the playground. Label 4 corners or areas with signs saying *ut*, *un*, *up* and *ug*. The students stand in the middle and when the teacher calls out a word containing one of these sounds, they must run to the matching corner. Try harder words, with more than one syllable, for example mutter, bunyip or struggle.

Related Reading Eggs Activities, Interactives, Songs and Books

Driving Tests

Test 3

Sight words:
are, not, his, her, we, very, me, be, to

Letters and sounds:
bug, to, at

Spelling Bank

Reading Eggs Library Books

Teacher Toolkit

Spelling Activities

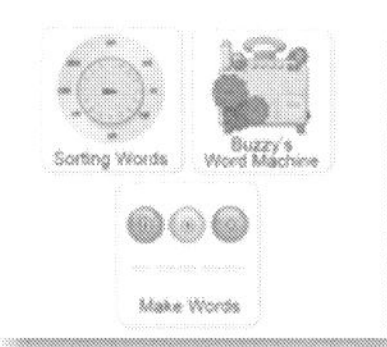

Grammar Lessons

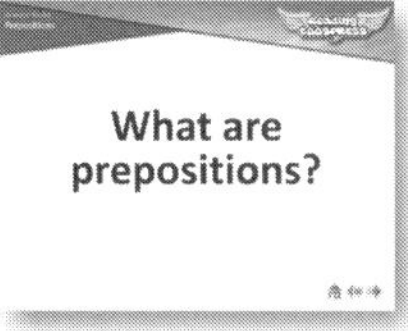

Reading Eggs Puzzle Park

More than One

Hidden Words

Song Lines

What is it?

My Program Books

Reading Eggs Apps

Eggy Sight words

Eggy Snap

Reading Eggs Posters

Critter Card

Flutter bye bye

Sight words

Lesson 64 • Worksheet 1

Name

1 Complete the dot to dot. Which word did you make?

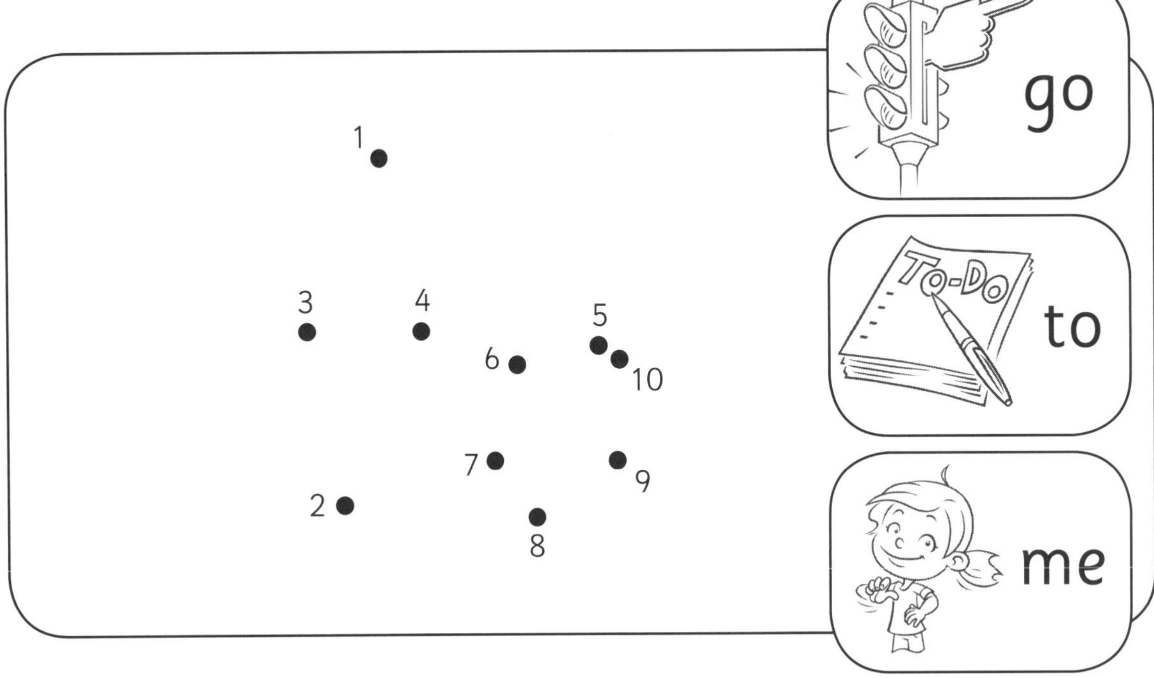

2 Find the words. Colour them in.

are you the said me to
her be very we his not

a	r	e	a	j	e	r	y	o	u	b	t	c
h	i	s	x	t	h	e	d	k	s	a	i	d
q	b	e	e	l	s	t	o	t	x	o	m	e
v	e	r	y	f	m	n	w	e	s	r	v	b
i	v	h	e	r	u	e	h	y	p	n	o	t

Name

Read and write

Lesson 64 • Worksheet 2

Complete each sentence with a word from the box.

Gus is a

-- .

Tubs is a

-- .

Tubs runs in the

-- .

The pup is stuck in the

-- .

Vocabulary

Lesson 64 • Worksheet 3

Name

1 Label the picture.

puppy duck mud

2 Read the questions and circle the answers.

Is the puppy muddy?	Yes	No
Is the duck stuck?	Yes	No
Is the puppy stuck?	Yes	No
Is it fun to be in the mud?	Yes	No
Does the duck run in the sun?	Yes	No
Does the pup run in the sun?	Yes	No

Name

Check

Lesson 64 · Worksheet 4

1 Trace and write the words.

at in

to on

2 Use the words above to complete the sentences.

I am ________ the castle.

We are ________ a ship.

Sid is ________ a hut.

Sam runs ________ his pup.

The pup likes ________ be in the mud.

Lesson 65 the sound **uck**

Learning objectives

Children will:

- read and write words using uck.
- identify rhyming words using uck.

Australian Curriculum Content Descriptions

Sound and letter knowledge

ACELA1439 listen to the sounds a student hears in the word, and write letters to represent those sounds; identify rhyme and syllables in spoken words; identify and manipulate sounds (phonemes) in spoken words

ACELA1440 identify familiar and recurring letters and the use of upper and lower case in written texts

Expressing and developing ideas

ACELA1435 learn that word order in sentences is important for meaning

ACELA1758 recognise the most common sound made by each letter of the alphabet, including consonants and short vowel sounds; write consonant-vowel-consonant words by writing letters to represent the sounds in the spoken words; know that spoken words are written down by listening to the sounds heard in the word and then writing letters to represent those sounds

Word families

duck, luck, muck, truck, stuck, suck, yuck

Vocabulary words

fluffy, drive

Extra assistance

The use of the double consonant *ck* for the sound /k/ can be confusing for students. It should be used after a short vowel sound, as in luck, lock, lick and lack. For some practise, have a Spelling Bee with /k/ words. The words could start with the /k/ sound, end with it, or have the /k/ sound in the middle. Some suggested words are: book, duck, chicken, looking, kitten, cat, like.

Classroom activities

Sentence Shuffle

Write and jumble an enlarged version of the sentence: Can Fluff the duck drive a truck? Read it with the children and ask them to work out the correct order. Reproduce each word on smaller pieces of card for each student. Suggest clues such as capital letters and question marks. Discuss the sentence when they are done.

Word Pairs

Give half the class a consonant on a card. Give the other half of the class a short u rime on a card. Ask the children to find a partner and sit together. Ask each consonant person to write their word on the board. Have the pairs swap cards and play again – they must make a different word this time!

Reading Eggs Lesson sequence	TEACH Content and skills	PRACTISE Children will:	APPLY
Hear: *Animated Lesson*	Introduce the word *duck*.	identify and read the word *duck* in a sentence.	**Worksheet 1** Word families
Write: *Make a Sentence*	Recognise correct word order for a sentence.	choose the correct words to make a sentence.	**Worksheet 2** Read and write
Find: *Alphabet Foods, Driving Trucks, Letter Lights*	Identify initial letters. Recognise a given word. Identify upper and lower case pairs of letters.	match pictures to their initial letter. Find the given word in a group. Match lower case letters to their capital.	**Worksheet 3** Vocabulary
Vocabulary: *Jigsaw, Word Windows, Fishing Boats, Tiles, Rhyme Time*	Build vocabulary skills: Recognise key vocabulary. Blend and recognise words. Identify rhyming words.	match pictures to words. Blend sounds to read and make words. Find rhyming words for *muck*.	**Worksheet 4** Check
Read: *Book Ends, Book*	Read sentences using basic vocabulary. Read aloud book.	choose from a list of words to finish the sentence. Listen, follow the reading and read along.	**Reading Eggs Story book** Fluff the duck

Related Reading Eggs Activities, Interactives, Songs and Books

Driving Tests

Spelling Bank

Reading Eggs Puzzle Park

More than One
Animal Fun
Transport
What is it?

Reading Eggs Posters

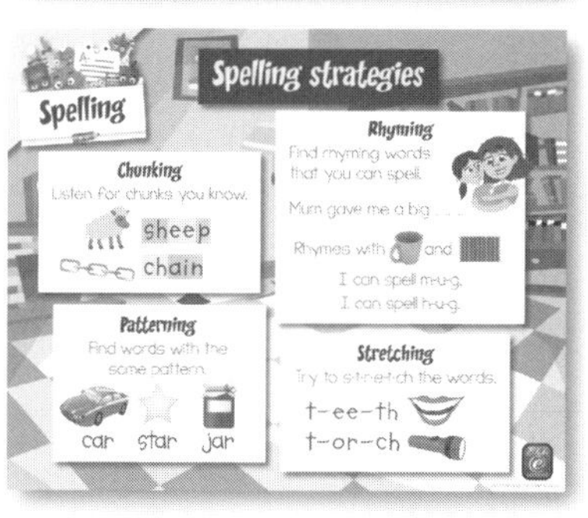

Reading Eggs Library Books

My Program Books

Critter Card

Fluff the duck

Teacher Toolkit

Spelling Activities

Reading Eggs Apps

Eggy Sight words

Eggy Snap

uck

Name

Word families

Lesson 65 • Worksheet 1

1 Join each word to a picture.

2 Circle the rhyming words in each row.

cut	mug	hut	pup	but
man	sun	bun	run	fin
luck	pack	yuck	suck	tick

Name

Read and write

Lesson 65 • Worksheet 2

1 Put the words in order to make each sentence.

duck muck.
stuck in
Fluff the
the gets

dog the
logs. gets
lots of
Tom

2 Write the rhyming words from each sentence.

Vocabulary

Lesson 65 • Worksheet 3

Name

Match the jigsaw pieces and write the words.
Draw a picture for each word you make.

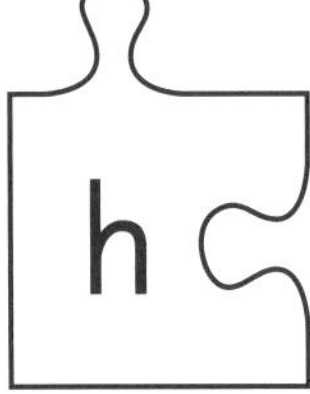

up ______________

ut ______________

ug ______________

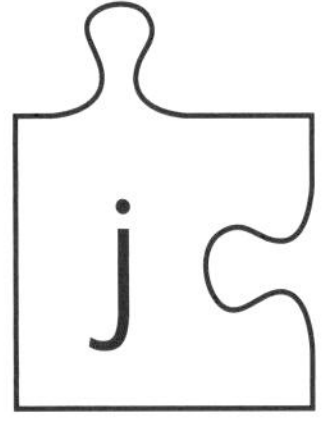

uck ______________

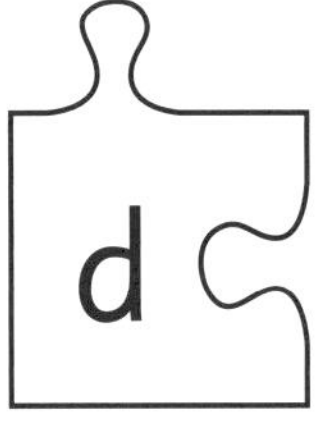

un ______________

Name

Check

Lesson 65 • Worksheet 4

1 Colour the right word. Cross out the wrong word.

truck

duck

muck

mug

puppy

yummy

duck

stuck

2 Complete the sentences using the words in the box.

in got mud truck see

Fluff got stuck in the ________.

Tom can ________ the bog.

He ________ lots of logs.

Fluff was ________ luck!

She can drive the ________.

Lesson 66 the words **there** and **that**

Learning objectives

Children will:

- identify the sight words there, that, hello and this.
- recognise the words leaf, mountain, branch and forest.

Australian Curriculum Content Descriptions

Sound and letter knowledge

ACELA1439 identify rhyme and syllables in spoken words; identify and manipulate sounds (phonemes) in spoken words

Expressing and developing ideas

ACELA1437 build vocabulary through multiple speaking and listening experiences

ACELA1758 recognise the most common sound made by each letter of the alphabet, including consonants and short vowel sounds; write consonant-vowel-consonant words by writing letters to represent the sounds in the spoken words, know that spoken words are written down by listening to the sounds heard in the word and then writing letters to represent those sounds

Interpreting, analysing and evaluating

ACELY1649 navigate a text correctly, starting at the right place and reading in the right direction, returning to the next line as needed, matching one spoken word to one written word

Sight words

there, that, this, hello

Vocabulary words

leaf, mountain, branch, forest, blue, yellow, red, green

Extra assistance

The sound /th/ does not exist in some languages, so students from these backgrounds may struggle to pronounce words like *there, that* and *this*. It can be mispronounced as /d/, /t/, /s/ or /f/. To help students practise this sound, have them stick their tongue out between the top and bottom teeth and then pull it away, exaggerating the movement to reinforce it.

Classroom activities

Memory Game

Write the word *forest* on the board. Sound it out with the class and discuss the recognisable chunks – *for* and *est*. Have students trace the word on someone's back or in the air with their finger. Rub out the word and write these words on the board: forrest, foreest, forist, forrist, forest. Ask them to identify which is correct, then discuss what is wrong with the other versions.

Colour Bingo!

Give students a laminated board with ten squares on it. Ask them to write a colour word in each square from the list: blue, yellow, red, green, black, pink (use whiteboard markers). Hold up items in various colours. Students put a cross on that colour word on their board. First one to ten calls out 'bingo' and wins!

Reading Eggs Lesson sequence	TEACH Content and skills	PRACTISE Children will:	APPLY
Hear: *Animated Lesson*	Introduce the words *there* and *that*.	identify and read the words *there* and *that* in isolation and in a sentence.	**Worksheet 1** Sight words
Write: *Missing Sound*	Identify the correct onset letter to complete the word.	choose the correct initial letter to make the word.	**Worksheet 2** Read and write
Find: *Word Sort, Frog Logs, Jumping Astronauts*	Identify starting and ending sounds. Recognise a given word.	sort words into boxes for start or end sounds. Find the given word in a group.	**Worksheet 3** Vocabulary
Vocabulary: *Rhyming Squares, Today's Words, Word Whiz, Jigsaw, Word Windows, Power Words*	Build vocabulary skills: Identify rhyming words. Recognise key vocabulary. Blend and recognise words.	find images of rhyming words. Tap on the word being said. Match pictures to words. Blend sounds to read words.	**Worksheet 4** Check
Read: *Book*	Read aloud book.	listen, follow the reading and read along.	**Reading Eggs Story book** Mountain top

Related Reading Eggs Activities, Interactives, Songs and Books

Driving Tests

Test 3

Sight words:
there, that, green, not

Letters and sounds:
leaf, bat, apple

Spelling Bank

Reading Eggs Puzzle Park

What is it?

Animal Colours

Colour Code

Do You Know?

Reading Eggs Posters

Reading Eggs Library Books

My Program Books

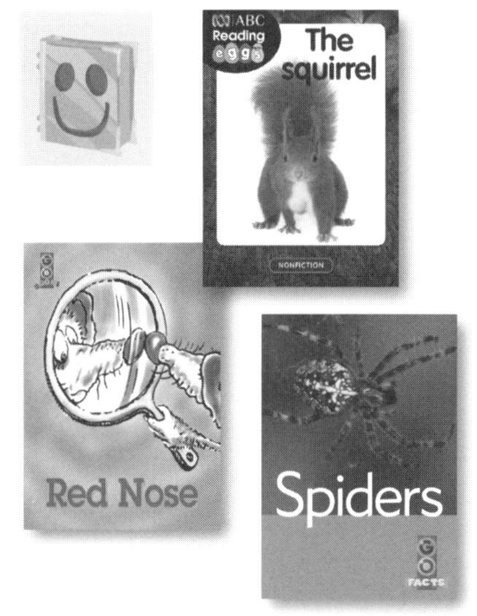

Critter Card

Mustard tops

Teacher Toolkit

Spelling Activities

Reading Eggs Apps

Eggy Sight words

Eggy Snap

there that

Lesson 66 • Worksheet 1

Name

Sight words

1 Trace and write the words.

there

that

this

2 Complete the sentences.

there That This

________ is a good bun.

Is he in ________ ?

________ is not a duck!

Name

Read and write

Lesson 66 • Worksheet 2

Put the words in order to make a sentence.

forest. big a was There

is a This leaf. green

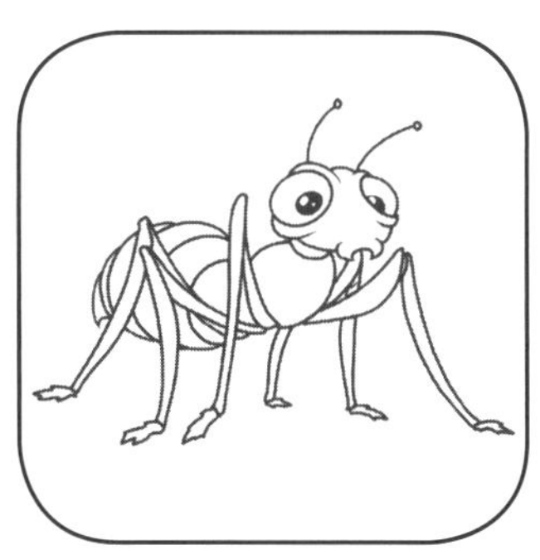

a is ant. That little

hello. Sam said the ant

Vocabulary

Lesson 66 · Worksheet 3

Name

1 Join each word to a picture.

2 Complete the sentences.

green big little tall

In the ________ forest there was a ________ tree. On a ________ leaf was a ________ ant.

Name

Check

Lesson 66 · Worksheet 4

Match the colour words to the items.
Draw and colour a picture of each.

yellow	apple
red	leaf
black	sun
green	sky
blue	bat

Lesson 67 the word **have**

Learning objectives

Children will:

- identify and read the word have.
- read and write words for facial features and colours.

Australian Curriculum Content Descriptions

Sound and letter knowledge

ACELA1439 listen to the sounds a student hears in the word, and write letters to represent those sounds; identify and manipulate sounds (phonemes) in spoken words

ACELA1440 identify familiar and recurring letters and the use of upper and lower case in written texts

Expressing and developing ideas

ACELA1435 learn that word order in sentences is important for meaning

ACELA1758 recognise the most common sound made by each letter of the alphabet, including consonants and short vowel sounds; know that spoken words are written down by listening to the sounds heard in the word and then writing letters to represent those sounds

Interpreting, analysing and evaluating

ACELY1649 navigate a text correctly, starting at the right place and reading in the right direction, returning to the next line as needed, matching one spoken word to one written word

Sight words

have

Vocabulary words

eyes, mouth, nose, chin, ears, hair, two, brown, blue, green

Extra assistance

A fun way to introduce new vocabulary is in themed lists, for example a list of facial features. This links the words in one definite context (the face), which can help students remember them more easily. It also lends itself to more visual/kinaesthetic learning as the words can be illustrated or demonstrated together in their context (for example, drawing and labelling or pointing to the features of a face).

Classroom activities

Make Your Own Sentences

Write this sentence on the board: I have _____ eyes.

Ask students to read this sentence by themselves, write it down and fill in the gap with the colour word to match their eyes. Then ask them to write a sentence about the person sitting next to or opposite them: He/She has _____ eyes.

Follow up with sentences about hair colour and ask students to draw, colour and label pictures of the two faces described.

Reading Eggs Lesson sequence	TEACH Content and skills	PRACTISE Children will:	APPLY
Vocabulary: *The Theme Game, Wheel of Words*	Build vocabulary skills: Recognise key vocabulary.	match pictures to words.	**Worksheet 1** Vocabulary
Write: *Look, Listen and Spell, Sound Streamers, Pick Up Bricks*	Identify sounds in a word and write the word. Recognise correct word order for a sentence.	sound out and select letters to spell a word correctly. Choose the correct words to make a sentence.	**Worksheet 2** Read and write
Find: *Leaping Penguins, Missing Sound, Trains*	Recognise a given word. Identify the correct onset letter to complete the word. Identify upper and lower case pairs of letters.	find the given word in a group. Choose the correct initial letter to make the word. Match lower case letters to their capital.	**Worksheet 3** Sight words
Match: *Read and Colour, Golden Goose*	Identify colour words. Recognise a given word.	use the correct colours. Find the given word in a group.	**Worksheet 4** Check
Read: *How Does it End?, Bubble Popper, Book*	Read sentences using basic vocabulary. Read aloud book.	read a beginning and match it to an ending. Read and follow instructions. Listen, follow the reading and read along.	**Reading Eggs Nonfiction** Eyes

Classroom activities

Bingo!

Give students a laminated board with ten squares on it. Ask them to write a word in each square from the list of facial features: mouth, eyes, nose, chin, hair, ears (use whiteboard markers). Point to your facial features or hold up pictures of the features. Students put a cross on that word on their board. First one to ten calls out 'bingo' and wins!

Related Reading Eggs Activities, Interactives, Songs and Books

Driving Tests

Test 2
Content words:
red, blue, brown, yellow, black, green

Spelling Bank

Reading Eggs Puzzle Park

More than One
Finish the Alien
Animal Colours
Colour Code

Reading Eggs Posters

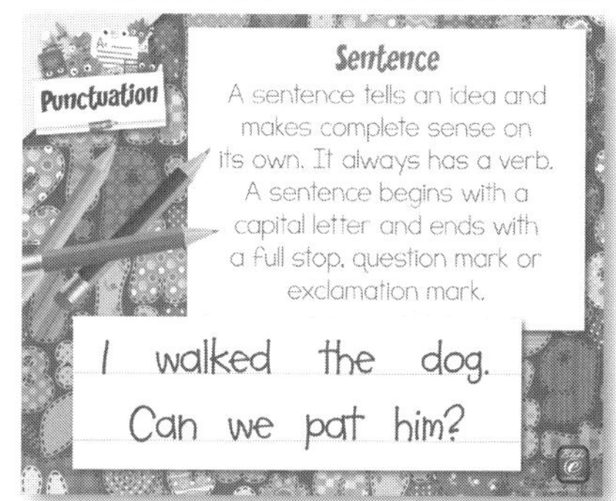

Reading Eggs Library Books

My Program Books

Critter Card

Gutter mutt

Teacher Toolkit

Spelling Activities

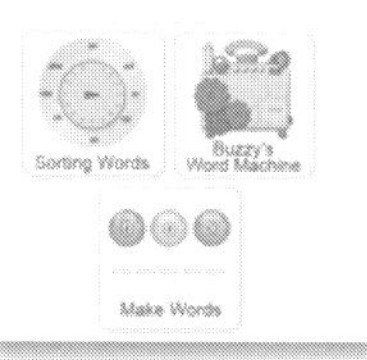

Reading Eggs Apps

Eggy Sight words

Eggy Snap

Vocabulary

Name

Lesson 67 • Worksheet 1

1 Complete the words for the parts of the face.

e_____es n_____se chi_____

ea_____s _____air mou_____h

2 Write the labels.

Name

Read and write

have

Lesson 67 • Worksheet 2

Finish each sentence using the numbers and pictures.

1 You have ______________

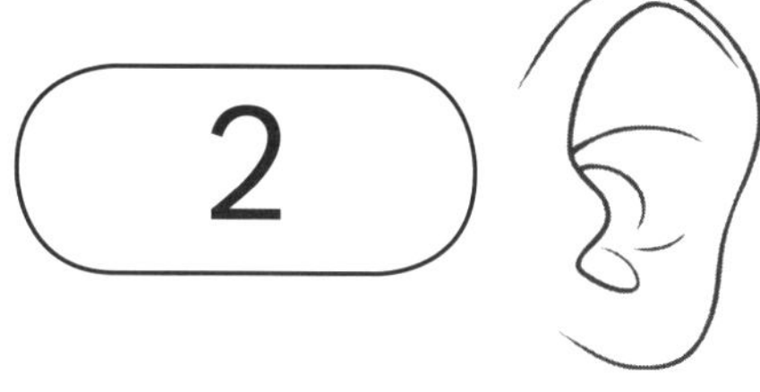
2 I have ______________

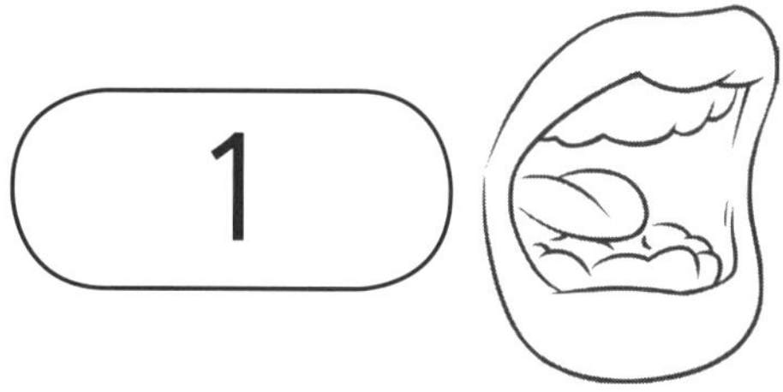
1 She has ______________

2 He has ______________

lots We have ________ of ________

1 I have ______________

have

Lesson 67 • Worksheet 3

Name

Sight words

1 Trace and write.

have

2 Circle the correct word. Cross out the wrong one.

I have has two eyes.

She have has one nose.

3 Match the number words, numerals and pictures.

one	2	
two	10	
ten	1	

Name

Check

Lesson 67 • Worksheet 4

1 Use the colour words to make these sentences about you.

red	black	brown	yellow
blue	green	pink	

My hair is _______________.

My eyes are _______________.

2 Crack the code and finish the face.

e = ●
r = ✿
u = ■
b = ▲
d = ★
a = ◗
c = ◆
l = ♥
k = ✚

▲♥■● eyes ✿●★ mouth

hair

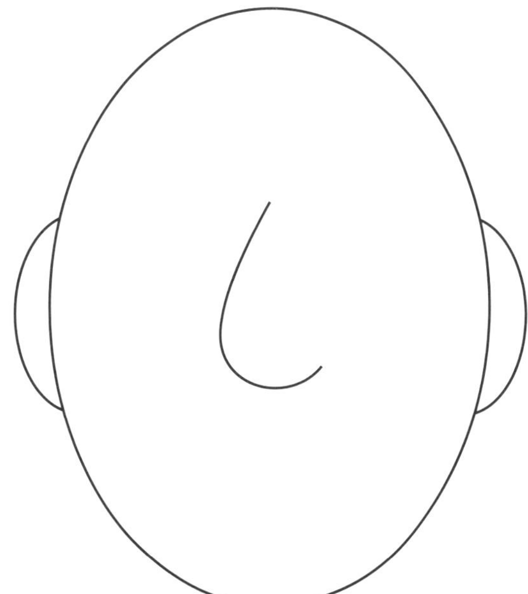

Lesson 68 the word **they**

Learning objectives

Children will:

- identify and read the word they.
- read and write words for body parts and numbers.

Australian Curriculum Content Descriptions

Sound and letter knowledge

ACELA1439 listen to the sounds a student hears in the word, and write letters to represent those sounds; identify and manipulate sounds (phonemes) in spoken words

Expressing and developing ideas

ACELA1435 learn that word order in sentences is important for meaning

ACELA1758 recognise the most common sound made by each letter of the alphabet, including consonants and short vowel sounds; write consonant-vowel-consonant words by writing letters to represent the sounds in the spoken words, know that spoken words are written down by listening to the sounds heard in the word and then writing letters to represent those sounds

Interpreting, analysing and evaluating

ACELY1649 navigate a text correctly, starting at the right place and reading in the right direction, returning to the next line as needed, matching one spoken word to one written word

Sight words

they, have

Vocabulary words

leg, eye, nose, dog, cat, one, two, three, four

Extra assistance

One way to make learning number words fun is to use songs involving numbers. In the Playroom on the Reading Eggs website is a Song Bookshelf which has animated versions of *1-2-3-4-5, 1-2 Buckle My Shoe, Five Little Ducks* and *Five Little Monkeys*. You could write out the lyrics and use them to make an illustrated book. Groups could act out the song or make short puppet plays.

Classroom activities

Sentence Shuffle

Write and jumble an enlarged version of the sentence: This is a cat and this is a dog. Read it with the children and ask them to work out the correct order. Reproduce each word on smaller pieces of card for each student. Suggest clues such as capital letters and full stops. Discuss the sentence when they are done.

How Many?

Put students in pairs or small groups and give them a sheet of paper with a number word written on it – *one, two* or *four.* Ask them to write or draw things that usually come in this number, eg 1 nose, 2 eyes, 4 legs on a dog. Bring the class together to share ideas.

Reading Eggs Lesson sequence	TEACH Content and skills	PRACTISE Children will:	APPLY
Hear: *Animated Lesson*	Introduce the word *they* using sentences and the song *I'm just a grub.*	identify and read the word *they* in isolation and in a sentence.	**Worksheet 1** Sight words
Write: *Make a Sentence, Look, Listen and Spell*	Recognise correct word order for a sentence. Identify sounds in a word and write the word.	choose the correct words to make a sentence. Sound out and select letters to spell a word correctly.	**Worksheet 2** Read and write
Find: *Squirter*	Recognise a given word.	find the given word in a group.	**Worksheet 3** Vocabulary
Vocabulary: *Word Windows, Fishing Boats, Break it Up, Jigsaw, Groups, Tiles*	Build vocabulary skills: Blend and recognise words. Recognise key vocabulary. Identify the number of phonemes in a word.	blend sounds to read and make words. Match pictures to words. Identify the number of sounds in a word.	**Worksheet 4** Check
Read: *Book Ends, Book*	Read sentences using basic vocabulary. Read aloud book.	choose from a list of words to finish the sentence. Listen, follow the reading and read along.	**Reading Eggs Nonfiction** Dogs and cats

Related Reading Eggs Activities, Interactives, Songs and Books

Driving Tests

Test 3

Sight words:
are, three, green, there, one, have, they

Letters and sounds:
cat, dog, leaf, bug

Content words:
one, two, three, four

Spelling Bank

Music Café

I'm just a grub

Reading Eggs Puzzle Park

More than One
Animal Fun
Finish the Alien
Fingers

Reading Eggs Posters

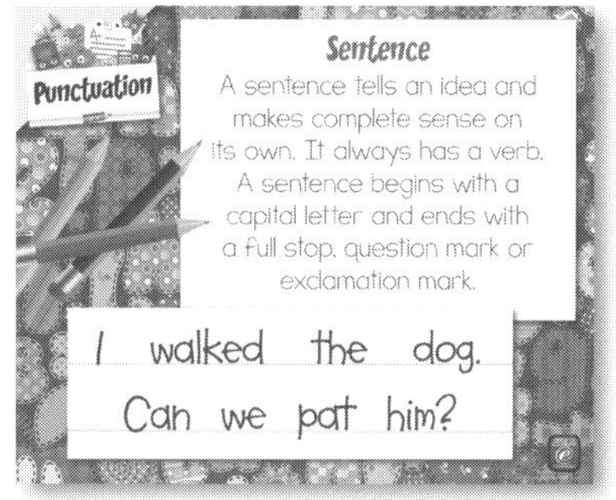

Reading Eggs Library Books

My Program Books

Critter Card

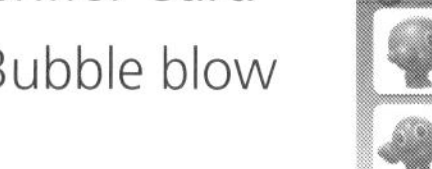

Bubble blow

Teacher Toolkit

Spelling Activities

Reading Eggs Apps

Eggy Sight words

Eggy Snap

Sight words

Lesson 68 • Worksheet 1

Name

1 Trace and write the words.

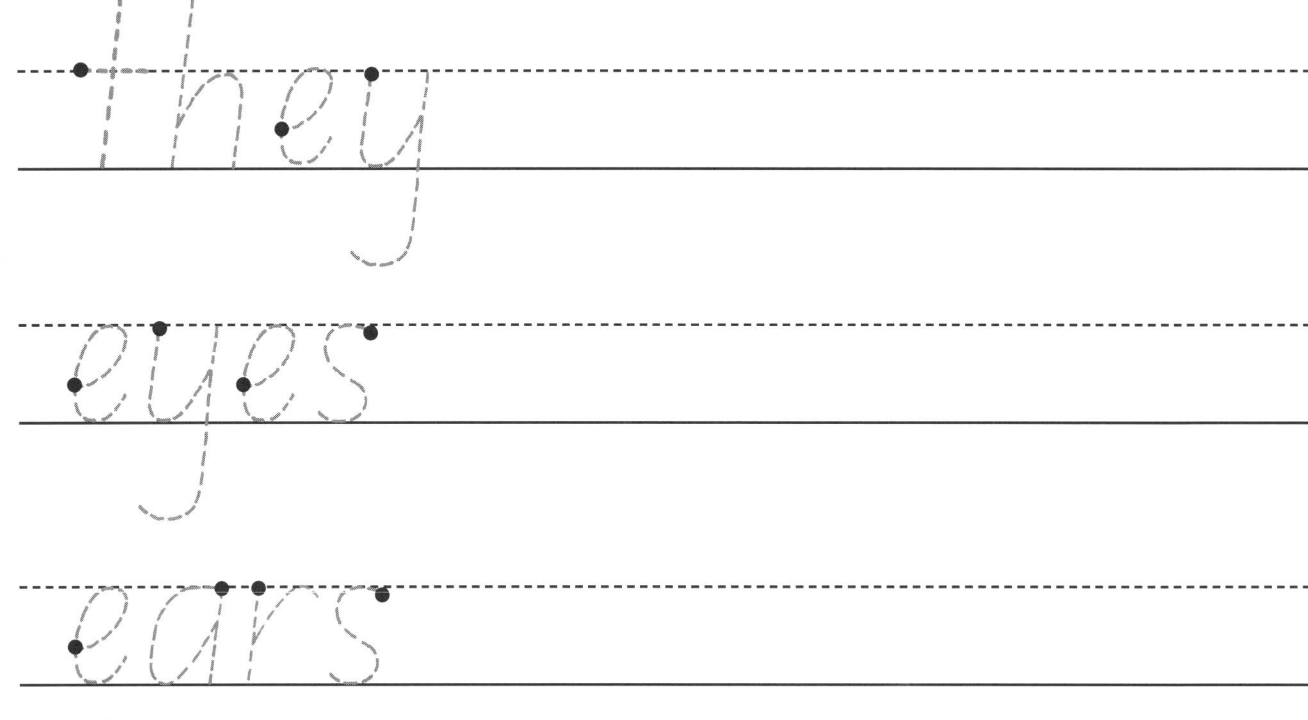

2 Use the words above to complete the sentences.

Tom the dog has two ________.

Jazz the cat has two ________.

They have four ________.

________ have one nose.

Name

Read and write

Lesson 68 · Worksheet 2

1 Colour the pictures.

2 Write four sentences about these people.

She ______________________________.

He ______________________________.

They ______________________________.

They ______________________________.

Vocabulary

Lesson 68 • Worksheet 3

Name

1 Read and draw.

A dog has four legs.	A cat has two eyes.
This is one leaf.	There are three bugs.

2 Match each number to a picture.

one

two

three

four

Name

Check

Lesson 68 • Worksheet 4

1 Colour the correct word. Cross out the wrong word.

Dogs have | two | four | legs.

Cats have two | eyes | legs | .

Hair can be | blue | brown | .

They have | one | two | eyes.

2 Find the words. Colour them in.

they have dog cat
leg nose eye ear

n	o	s	e	j	w	r	y	o	u	d	o	g
h	i	t	h	e	y	m	d	k	e	a	r	c
q	l	e	g	l	s	t	e	y	e	l	t	w
c	a	t	y	f	m	n	b	l	h	a	v	e

Lesson 69 the word **do**

Learning objectives

Children will:

- identify and read the word do.
- read and write using verbs.

Australian Curriculum Content Descriptions

Sound and letter knowledge

ACELA1439 listen to the sounds a student hears in the word, and write letters to represent those sounds; identify rhyme and syllables in spoken words; identify and manipulate sounds (phonemes) in spoken words

Expressing and developing ideas

ACELA1435 learn that word order in sentences is important for meaning

ACELA1758 recognise the most common sound made by each letter of the alphabet, including consonants and short vowel sounds; know that spoken words are written down by listening to the sounds heard in the word and then writing letters to represent those sounds

Interpreting, analysing and evaluating

ACELY1649 navigate a text correctly, starting at the right place and reading in the right direction, returning to the next line as needed, matching one spoken word to one written word

Sight words

do, can, cannot

Vocabulary words

jump, grin, swim, fly, run

Extra assistance

In English we always end a sentence with a punctuation mark – usually a full stop, a question mark or an exclamation mark. Students need to know when to use these correctly. A question is usually easy for students to distinguish. An exclamation mark should be used when high emotions are involved – fear, anger, excitement, awe, surprise. This is harder for students to understand. Give them opportunities to write exclamations and point out exclamation marks in reading materials.

Classroom activities

Rhyme Time

Write the word *sun* on the board and ask students to suggest rhyming words which are written underneath. Give small groups a sheet of paper with a word written at the top and ask them to fill the sheet with rhyming words. Use short *u* sound words – bug, cut, cup, duck. Bring the class back together to share their words.

Can or Cannot?

Sit students in a circle and give each child a card that has *can* on one side and *cannot* on the other side. Ask the class questions that can be answered with *can* or *cannot*, for example, Can a cat say the alphabet? They hold up their card to show their answer. You could also ask students to take turns asking a question. Discuss any question that elicits a mixed response.

Reading Eggs Lesson sequence	**TEACH Content and skills**	**PRACTISE Children will:**	**APPLY**
Hear: *Animated Lesson*	Introduce the word *do*.	identify and read the word *do* in isolation and in a sentence.	**Worksheet 1** Sight words
Write: *Pick Up Bricks*	Recognise correct word order for a sentence.	choose the correct words to make a sentence.	**Worksheet 2** Read and write
Find: *Alphabet Foods, Rhyming Squares*	Identify initial letters. Recognise rhyming words.	match pictures to their initial letter. Find images of rhyming words.	**Worksheet 3** Vocabulary
Vocabulary: *Blend a Word, Jigsaw, Make a Word, Word Dominoes, Break it Up, Power Words*	Build vocabulary skills: Blend and recognise words. Recognise key vocabulary. Identify initial letters by sound and read written words. Identify the number of phonemes in a word.	blend sounds to read words. Match pictures to words. Match pictures to their initial letter. Identify the number of sounds in a word.	**Worksheet 4** Check
Read: *Book Ends, Book*	Read sentences using basic vocabulary. Read aloud book.	choose from a list of words to finish the sentence. Listen, follow the reading and read along.	**Reading Eggs Story book** Run and jump

Related Reading Eggs Activities, Interactives, Songs and Books

Driving Tests

Spelling Bank

Reading Eggs Puzzle Park

Hidden Words
Song Lines
Do it
What is it?

Reading Eggs Posters

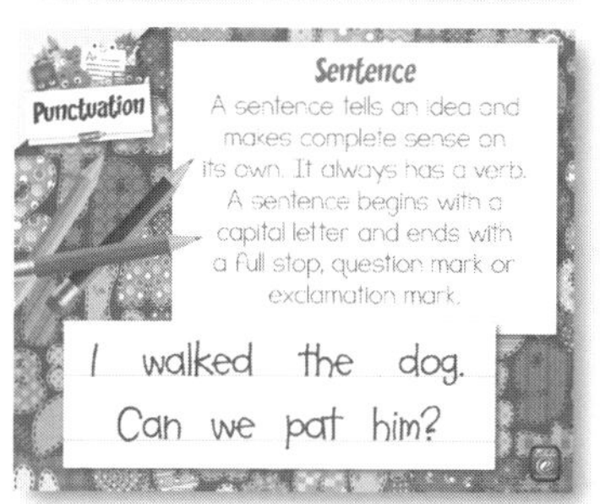

Reading Eggs Library Books

My Program Books

Critter Card

Gus the dump truck

Teacher Toolkit

Spelling Activities

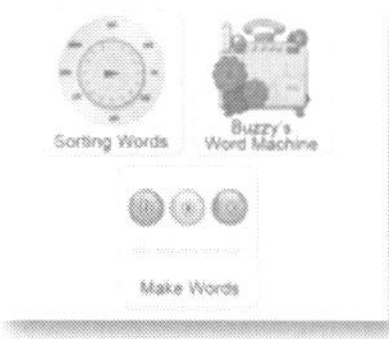

Grammar Lessons

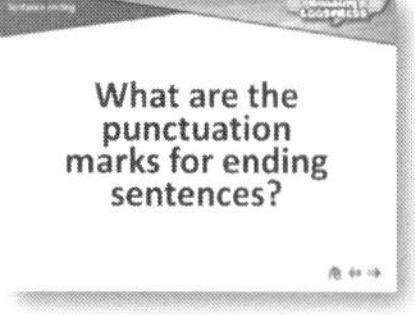

Reading Eggs Apps

Eggy Sight words

Eggy Snap

do

Lesson 69 • Worksheet 1

Name

Sight words

1 Trace and write.

2 Folow the path of **do** words to get Gus the dump truck to his job.

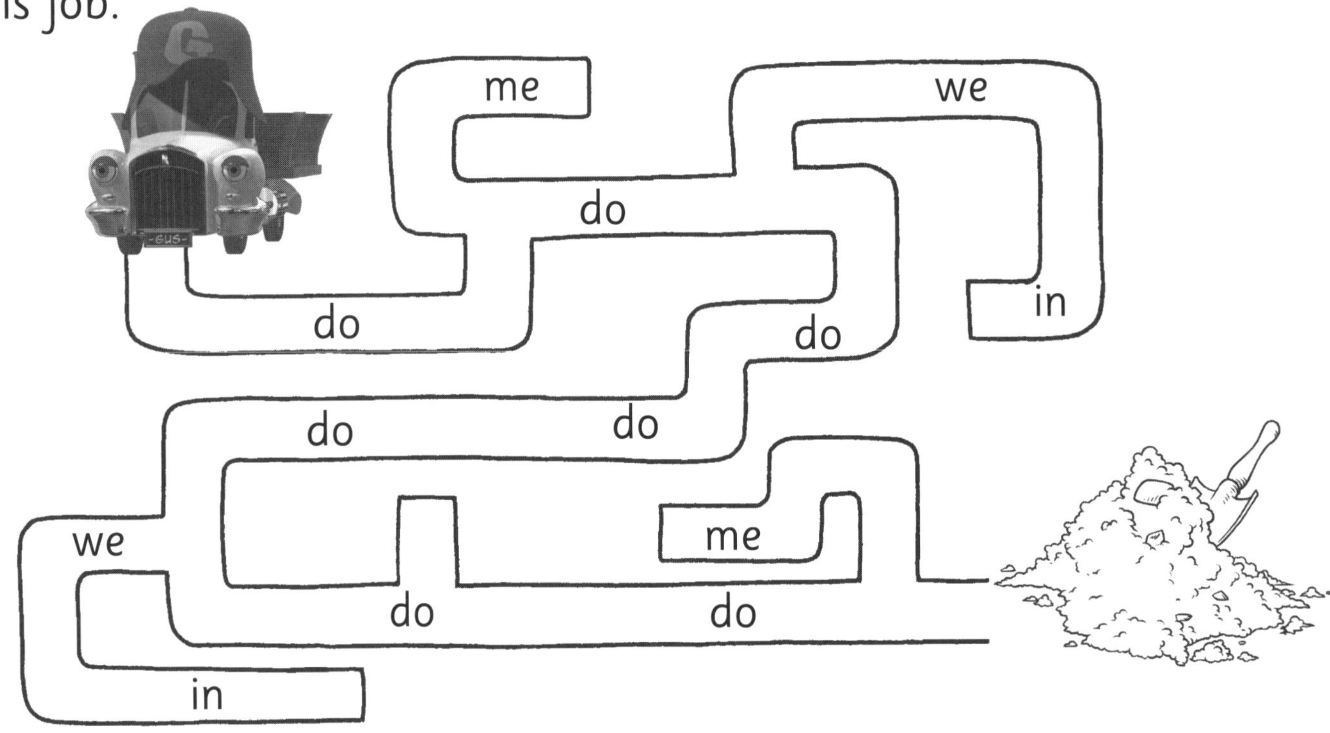

3 Add **Do** and answer the questions.

________ you like bugs? Yes No

________ you run fast? Yes No

________ you eat apples? Yes No

Name

Read and write

Lesson 69 • Worksheet 2

1 Complete each sentence with a word from the box.

jump swim run

Fluff the duck can ________.

Frogfish can ________.

Tom the dog can ________.

2 Write a sentence about you. Draw a picture.

I can

Vocabulary

Name

Lesson 69 • Worksheet 3

1 Join each word to a picture.

2 Colour the **verbs** – the doing words.

run	bug	blue	dog	swim
cat	we	jump	one	green
I	skip	sun	fly	grin

3 Tick the things you can do.

jump ☐ fly ☐ run ☐

skip ☐ swim ☐ grin ☐

Name

Check

Lesson 69 · Worksheet 4

1 Match the jigsaw pieces and write the words.

2 Colour the correct word. Cross out the wrong one.

Sam the ant can cannot fly.

Frogfish can cannot jump.

Fluff the duck can cannot swim.

Tom the dog can cannot buzz.

Lesson 70 Review

Learning objectives

Children will:

- read and write words using the short /u/ sound.
- recognise known verbs and sight words.

Australian Curriculum Content Descriptions

Sound and letter knowledge

ACELA1439 listen to the sounds a student hears in the word, and write letters to represent those sounds; identify and manipulate sounds (phonemes) in spoken words

ACELA1440 identify familiar and recurring letters and the use of upper and lower case in written texts

Expressing and developing ideas

ACELA1758 recognise the most common sound made by each letter of the alphabet, including consonants and short vowel sounds; know that spoken words are written down by listening to the sounds heard in the word and then writing letters to represent those sounds

Interpreting, analysing and evaluating

ACELY1649 navigate a text correctly, starting at the right place and reading in the right direction, returning to the next line as needed, matching one spoken word to one written word

Word families

ug, un, ut, ub, uck

Vocabulary words

bus

Extra assistance

Students who speak a language other than English may have trouble distinguishing between the short vowel sounds. Use consonant-vowel-consonant words to reinforce vowel sounds. Give students a list of words with the vowels missing. Say the words out loud and students fill in the middle sound. This is a good way to assess who is having trouble distinguishing them.

Classroom activities

Word Pairs

Give half the class a consonant on a card and the other half a short u rime on a card. Ask the children to find a partner to make a word and sit together. Each consonant person writes their word on the board. Have the pairs swap cards and play again – they must make a different word this time!

Bingo!

Give students a laminated board with ten squares on it. Ask them to write a word in each square from the list: *me, be, to, there, that, this, have, they, do, run, jump, fly* (use whiteboard markers). Say words from the list. Students put a cross on that word on their board. First one to ten calls out 'bingo' and wins!

Reading Eggs Lesson sequence	TEACH Content and skills	PRACTISE Children will:	APPLY
Write: *Word Ladder*	Identify sounds in a word and write the word.	sound out a word and select letters to spell it correctly.	**Worksheet 1** Word families
Find: *1, 2, 3, 4, Time for 20*	Identify the order of a sequence of events. Recognise a given word.	put pictures in order to show a sequence of events. Find the given word in a group.	**Worksheet 2** Sight words
Match: *Letter Lights, What's Missing?*	Identify upper and lower case pairs of letters. Match the missing sound to its word.	match lower case letters to their capital. Choose the correct letter to finish the word.	**Worksheet 3** Vocabulary
Vocabulary: *Words per Minute, Make a Monster, Find Your Treasure, Word Windows, Power Words*	Build vocabulary skills: Recognise key vocabulary. Blend and recognise words.	match pictures to words. Read and follow instructions. Blend sounds to read words.	**Worksheet 4** Check
Read: *Book Ends, Book*	Read sentences using basic vocabulary. Read aloud book.	choose from a list of words to finish the sentence. Listen, follow the reading and read along.	**Reading Eggs book** Word families for ug, un, ut, ub, uck

Related Reading Eggs Activities, Interactives, Songs and Books

Driving Tests

Map 3

Lessons 17 – 20

Focus sound words: short u words

High frequency sight words: one, do, me, us, see

Challenge: short u words

Reading Eggs Puzzle Park

Animal Fun

Finish the Alien

Colour Code

Do it

Squares

Spelling Bank

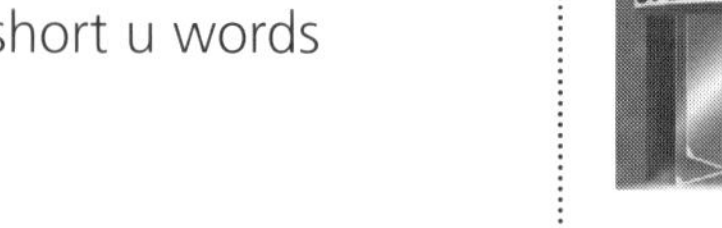

Reading Eggs Posters

Reading Eggs Library Books

My Program Books

Critter Card

Bunky boo

Teacher Toolkit

Spelling Activities

Reading Eggs Apps

Eggy Sight words

Eggy Snap

Eggy Phonics 1

Review

Lesson 70 · Worksheet 1

Name

Word families

Sort these words into their word families.

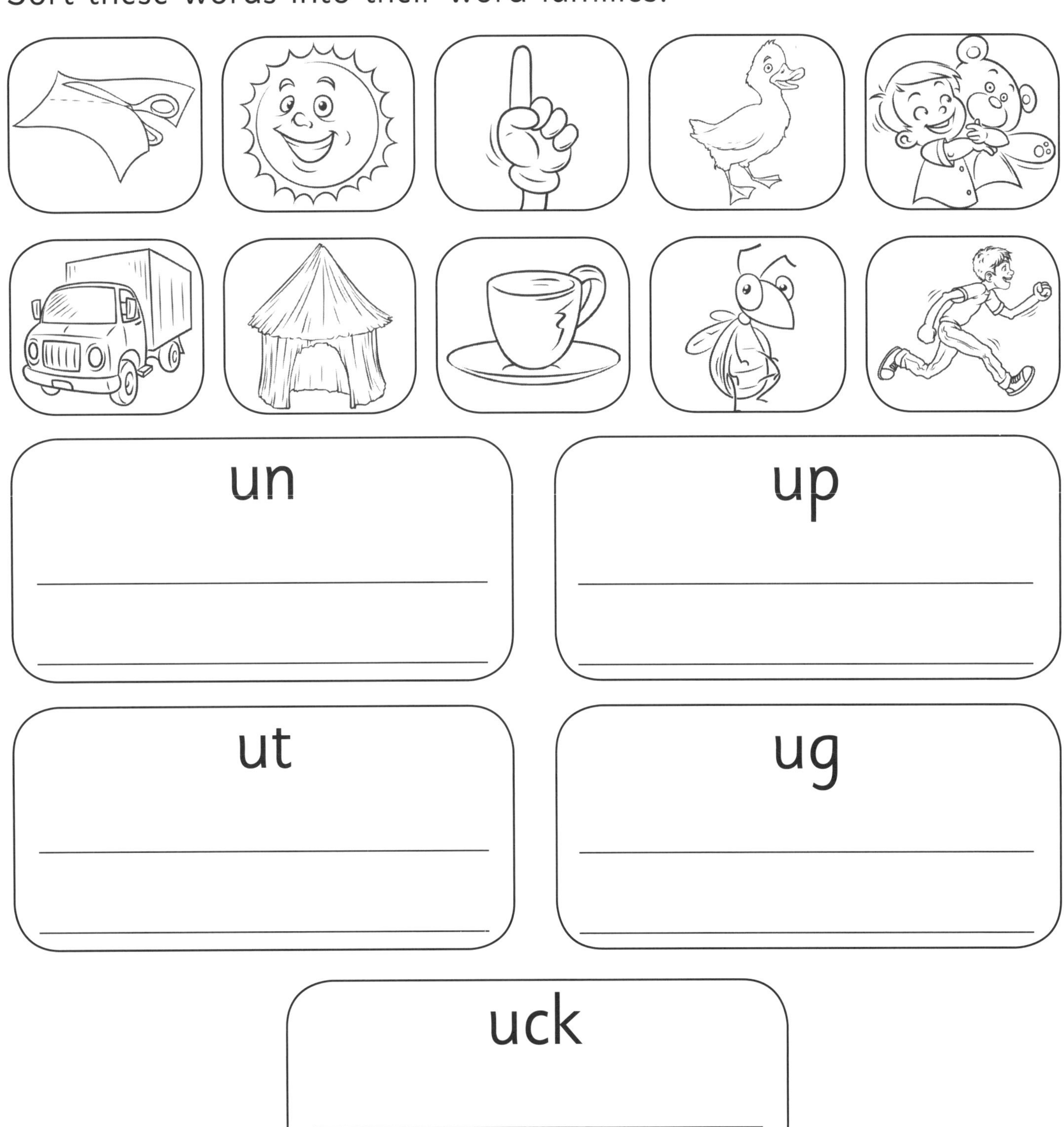

Name

Review

Lesson 70 • Worksheet 2

Sight words

1 Complete each sentence using a word from the box.

They There that This have

I __________ two bugs.

__________ are green.

__________ is a cat.

__________ cat is black.

Look at __________ black cat!

2 Colour the correct word. Cross out the wrong word.

Do | To you run?

Look at me | be.

We can go to | do the park.

I will me | be there!

Review

Lesson 70 • Worksheet 3

Name

Vocabulary

1 Match numbers to items.

2 Match colours to items.

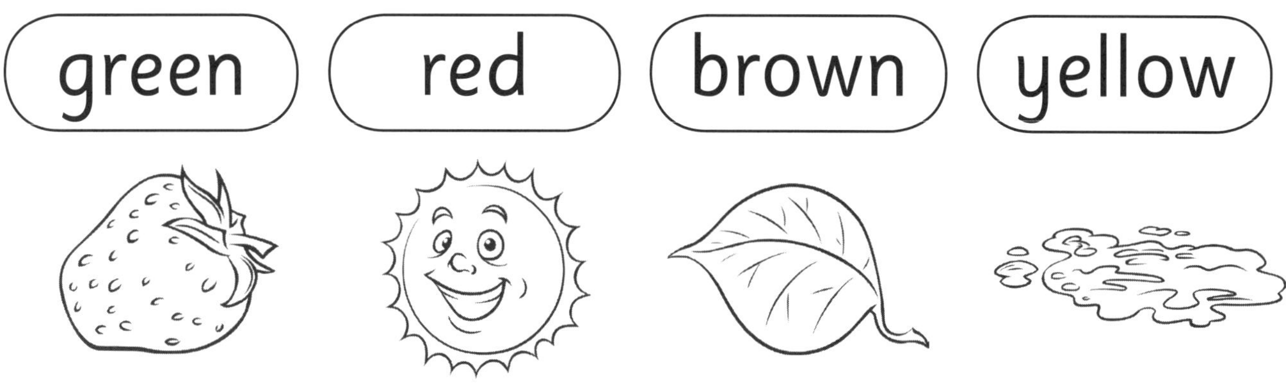

3 Join each word to a picture.

Name

Check

Review

Lesson 70 • Worksheet 4

1 Draw three bugs, two nuts and one cup.

2 Write a sentence using these words.

dog legs muddy

3 Colour two balloons red, three balloons blue and one balloon green.

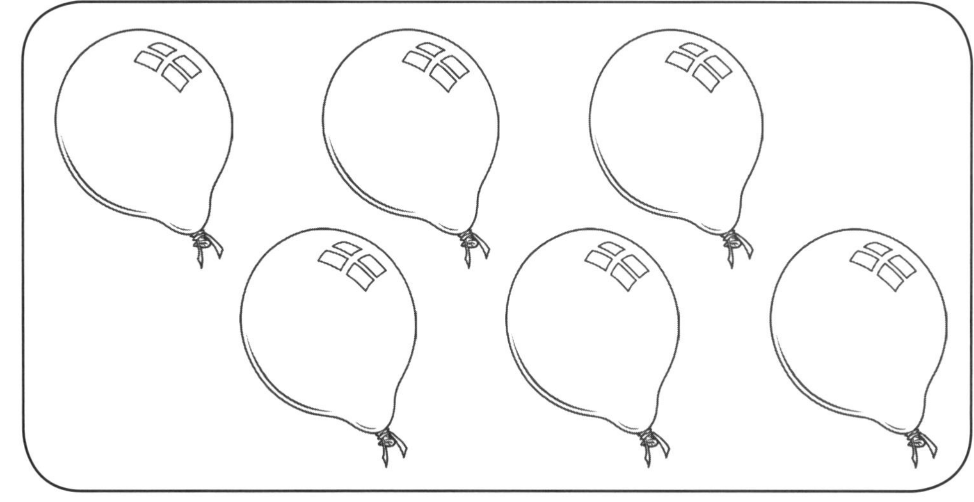

Lesson 71 the words **my, come** and **play**

Learning objectives

Children will:

- identify the words my, come, play, goes.
- read and write words from a party theme.

Australian Curriculum Content Descriptions

Sound and letter knowledge

ACELA1439 listen to the sounds a student hears in the word, and write letters to represent those sounds; identify and manipulate sounds (phonemes) in spoken words

Expressing and developing ideas

ACELA1435 learn that word order in sentences is important for meaning

ACELA1758 recognise the most common sound made by each letter of the alphabet, including consonants and short vowel sounds; write consonant-vowel-consonant words by writing letters to represent the sounds in the spoken words; know that spoken words are written down by listening to the sounds heard in the word and then writing letters to represent those sounds

Interpreting, analysing and evaluating

ACELY1649 navigate a text correctly, starting at the right place and reading in the right direction, returning to the next line as needed, matching one spoken word to one written word

Sight words

my, come, play, goes

Vocabulary words

chair, people, plate, table, band, food, day

Extra assistance

In the present tense, some verbs change form. For example:

Here *come* the tables.	They *play* together.
Here *comes* the table.	He *plays* alone.

The verbs *come, go* and *play* introduced in this lesson, can provide some clear examples for teaching students to add *s* to the verb when the subject is singular.

Classroom activities

Sentence Shuffle

Write and jumble an enlarged version of the sentence: Here come the people. Read it with the children and ask them to work out the correct order. Reproduce each word on smaller pieces of card for each student. Suggest clues such as capital letters and full stops. Discuss the sentence when they are done.

Make Your Own Story

Students use their own theme words to complete the sentence: Here come the ... If they are able, ask them to do this multiple times to create a story of their own. Suggested themes are the zoo, the farm, the pet show, the circus, the carnival, at school or on the road. Students could illustrate each sentence and make a little book.

Reading Eggs Lesson sequence	**TEACH Content and skills**	**PRACTISE Children will:**	**APPLY**
Hear: *Animated Lesson*	Introduce the words *my, come* and *play* and watch the song *Sid and Jazz bounce on.*	identify and read the words *my, come* and *play* in isolation and in a sentence.	**Worksheet 1** Sight words
Write: *Ball Game, Tiles, Make a Sentence*	Identify sounds in a word and write the word. Recognise correct word order for a sentence.	sound out a word and select letters to spell it correctly. Choose the correct words to make a sentence.	**Worksheet 2** Read and write
Find: *Frog Logs, Squirter, Shooting Stars*	Recognise a given word.	find the given word in a group.	**Worksheet 3** Vocabulary
Vocabulary: *Jigsaw, The Theme Game, Blend a Word, Wheel of Words, Break it Up*	Build vocabulary skills: Recognise key vocabulary. Blend and recognise words. Identify the number of phonemes in a word.	match pictures to words. Blend sounds to read words. Identify the number of sounds in a word.	**Worksheet 4** Check
Read: *Book*	Read aloud book.	listen, follow the reading and read along.	**Reading Eggs Story book** The picnic

Related Reading Eggs Activities, Interactives, Songs and Books

Driving Tests

Test 4

Sight words:

come, my, goes, day

Spelling Bank

Music Café

Sid and Jazz bounce on

Reading Eggs Puzzle Park

More than One

Hidden Words

Song Lines

Do it

Reading Eggs Library Books

My Program Books

Reading Eggs Posters

Teacher Toolkit

Spelling Activities

Grammar Lessons

Reading Eggs Apps

Eggy Sight words

Eggy Snap

Critter Card

Eggster

come play

Lesson 71 • Worksheet 1

Name

Sight words

1 Trace and write.

come play

2 Use the correct form of the verbs to complete the sentences.

come comes play plays

I will ___________ to the party.

You can ___________ in the sun.

Here ___________ the food.

Sid ___________ in the band.

Name

my come play

Lesson 71 • Worksheet 2

Read and write

Finish each sentence with a word from the box and draw a picture.

goes   my   comes   plays

The boy ________ to a party.

The dog ________ at the park.

Here ________ the bus.

I like ________ bag.

Vocabulary

Name

Lesson 71 • Worksheet 3

1 Join each word to a picture.

2 Follow the instructions to draw a party.

- 1 table
- 3 chairs
- 6 people
- lots of food

Colour in.

Name

Check

Lesson 71 • Worksheet 4

1 How many sounds can you hear in each word? Colour the box.

my	goes	food
1 2 3 4	1 2 3 4	1 2 3 4
band	**plate**	**table**
1 2 3 4	1 2 3 4	1 2 3 4

2 Circle the party words.

band dog the food king
come people you goes chairs

3 Write each word in the matching boxes.

my
people
goes
plate
food

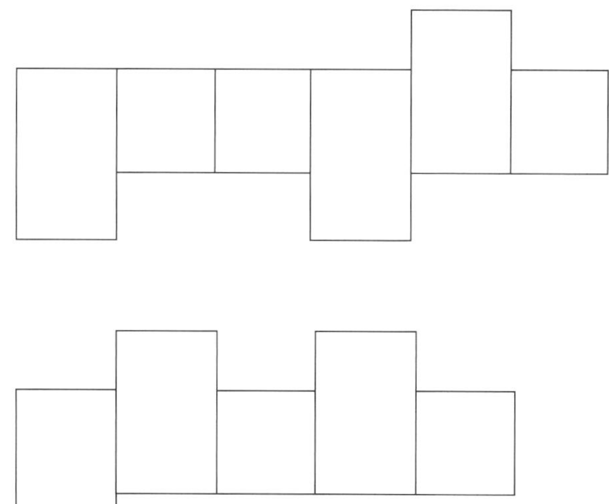

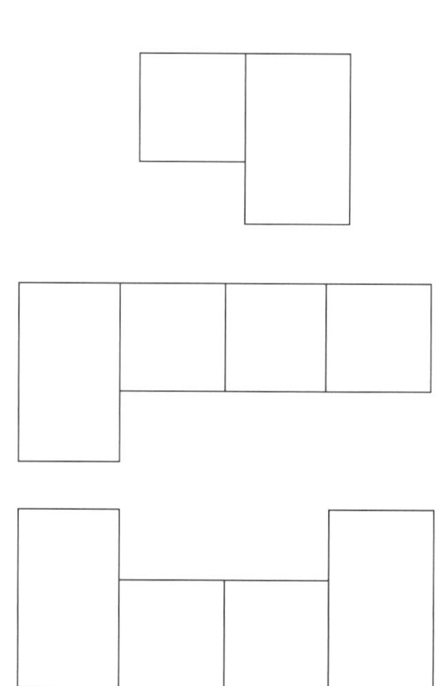

Lesson 72 the sounds **ed** and **eg**

Learning objectives

Children will:

- read and write ed and eg words.
- recognise verbs ending with ing.

Australian Curriculum Content Descriptions

Sound and letter knowledge

ACELA1439 listen to the sounds a student hears in the word, and write letters to represent those sounds; identify and manipulate sounds (phonemes) in spoken words

Creating texts

ACELY1653 follow clear demonstrations of how to construct each letter, learn to construct lower case letters

Expressing and developing ideas

ACELA1435 learn that word order in sentences is important for meaning

ACELA1438 build word families using onset and rime

ACELA1758 recognise the most common sound made by each letter of the alphabet, including consonants and short vowel sounds; write consonant-vowel-consonant words by writing letters to represent the sounds in the spoken words; know that spoken words are written down by listening to the sounds heard in the word and then writing letters to represent those sounds

Word families

bed, red, leg, peg, beg, egg

Vocabulary words

dinosaur, cracking, rolling, breaking, open, baby, hello

Extra assistance

Verbs end with *–ing* when they need to do something other than be a verb. In this lesson they are the object of the sentence, not the verb. For example, The egg is cracking. The egg is the subject, the verb is *is* and the object is *cracking*.

At this stage it is easiest to explain to students that you need a short verb in front of an *–ing* verb, eg I *am going*, they *are playing*, she *is running*. Give students activities to practise this idea, using the verbs *is, are* and *am* with an *–ing* word to describe what is happening.

Classroom activities

How Does it End?

Put the letters *b, f, l, p, r* and *w* on the board in magnetic letters. Put the sounds *ed* and *eg* on the board. Each student comes to the board and makes a word using an initial letter and an ending. Discuss their words with the class.

End it!

Put a list of words on the board and ask students if you can put *–ing* on the end. Use singular and plural nouns, verbs and adjectives. Get students to try putting them in a sentence. See if the children can explain why some words work and some don't.

Reading Eggs Lesson sequence	**TEACH Content and skills**	**PRACTISE Children will:**	**APPLY**
Hear: *Animated Lesson*	Introduce the sound *ed* through the song *Jazz thinks ed.*	identify the *ed* sound.	**Worksheet 1** Word families
Write: *Dot-to-dot, Sound Streamers, Tiles, Pick Up Bricks*	Reinforce correct letter formation. Identify sounds in words. Recognise correct word order for a sentence.	write the word *bed*. Sound out and select letters to make words. Choose the correct words to make a sentence.	**Worksheet 2** Read and write
Find: *Driving Trucks, Word family*	Recognise a given word. Identify the correct onset letter to complete the word.	find the given word in a group. Choose the correct initial letter to make the word.	**Worksheet 3** Vocabulary
Vocabulary: *Today's Words, The Theme Game, Words per Minute*	Build vocabulary skills: Recognise key vocabulary.	tap on the word being said. Match pictures to words.	**Worksheet 4** Check
Read: *How does it end?, Book*	Read sentences using basic vocabulary. Read aloud book.	read a beginning and match it to the correct ending. Listen, follow the reading and read along.	**Reading Eggs Story book** The dinosaur egg

Related Reading Eggs Activities, Interactives, Songs and Books

Driving Tests

Map 1

Lesson 6

Focus sound words: bed, fed, red, wed, peg, beg, legs

Challenge: shed, egg

Spelling Bank

Music Café

Jazz thinks ed

Reading Eggs Puzzle Park

More than One

Hidden Words

Song Lines

Do it

Reading Eggs Posters

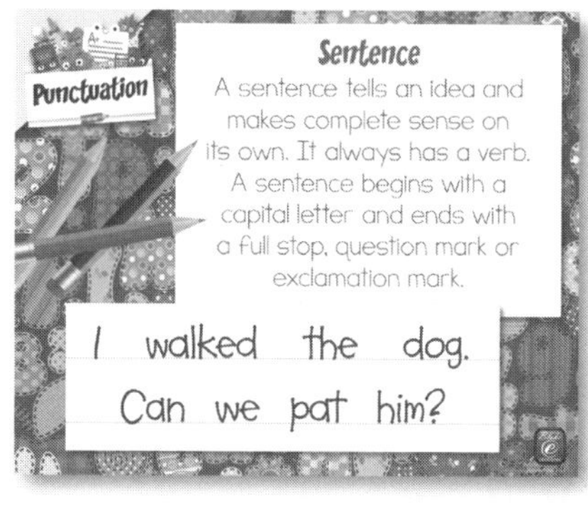

Reading Eggs Library Books

My Program Books

Critter Card

Penny drop

Teacher Toolkit

Spelling Activities

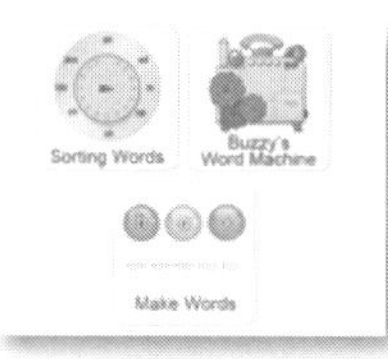

Reading Eggs Apps

Eggy Sight words

Eggy Snap

Eggy Phonics 1

ed eg

Lesson 72 • Worksheet 1

Name

Word families

1 Put the letters through the word machines. Write the words you make.

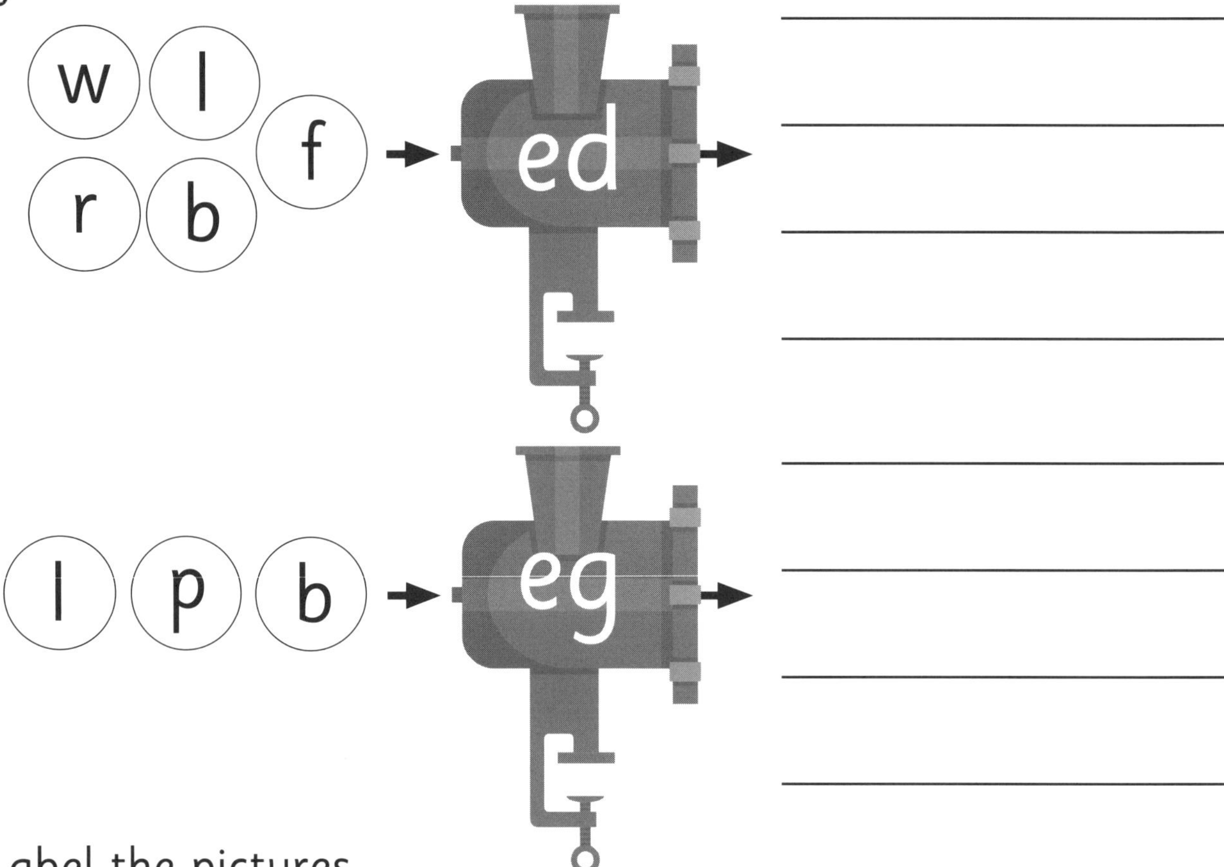

2 Label the pictures.

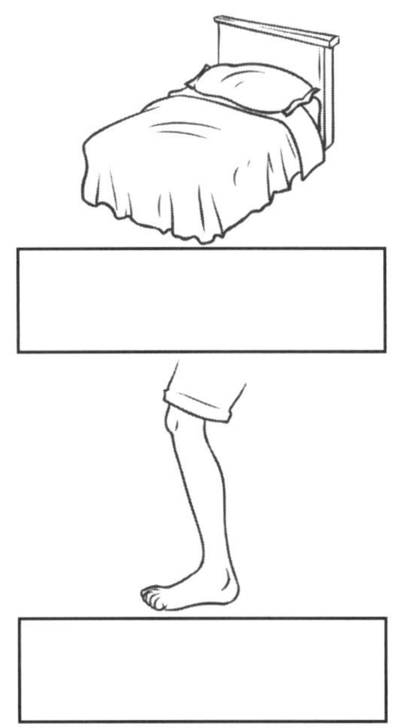

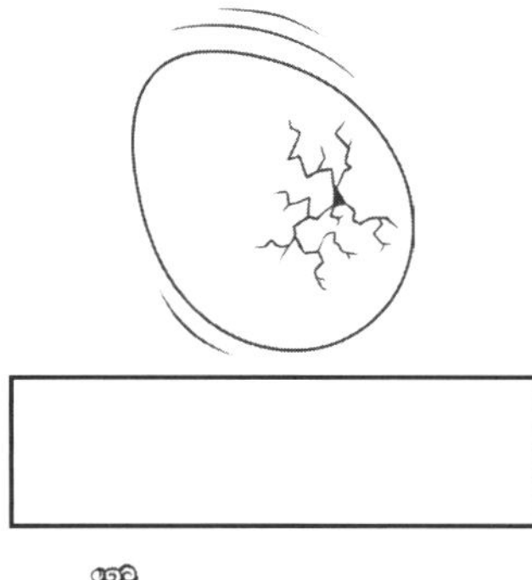

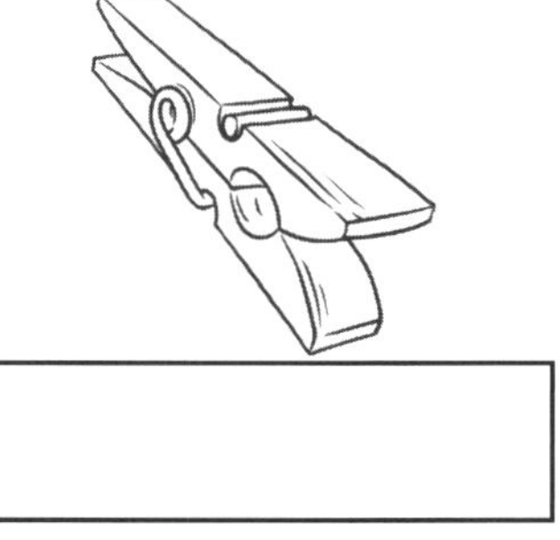

Name

Read and write

Lesson 72 • Worksheet 2

1 Put the words in the correct order to make a sentence.

dinosaur This a egg. is

egg is The green. dinosaur

2 Draw a picture for the sentences above.

Vocabulary

Name

Lesson 72 • Worksheet 3

1 Add **ing** to each word.

do________ roll________

crack________ bang________

jump________ break________

2 Complete the sentences with words from above.

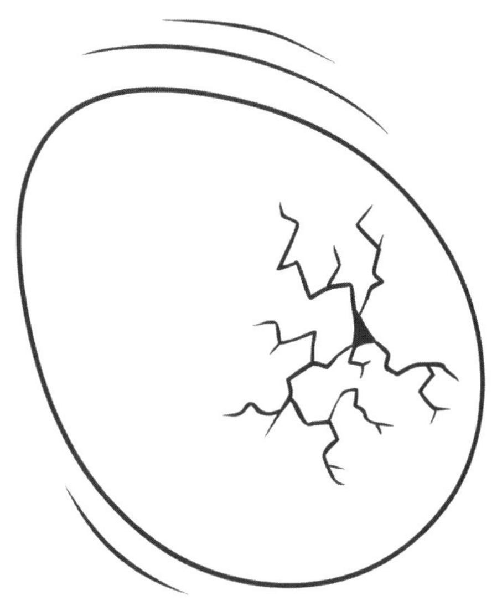

The dinosaur egg is

________________.

The dinosaur egg is

________________.

Name

Check

ed eg

Lesson 72 · Worksheet 4

1 Join each word to a picture.

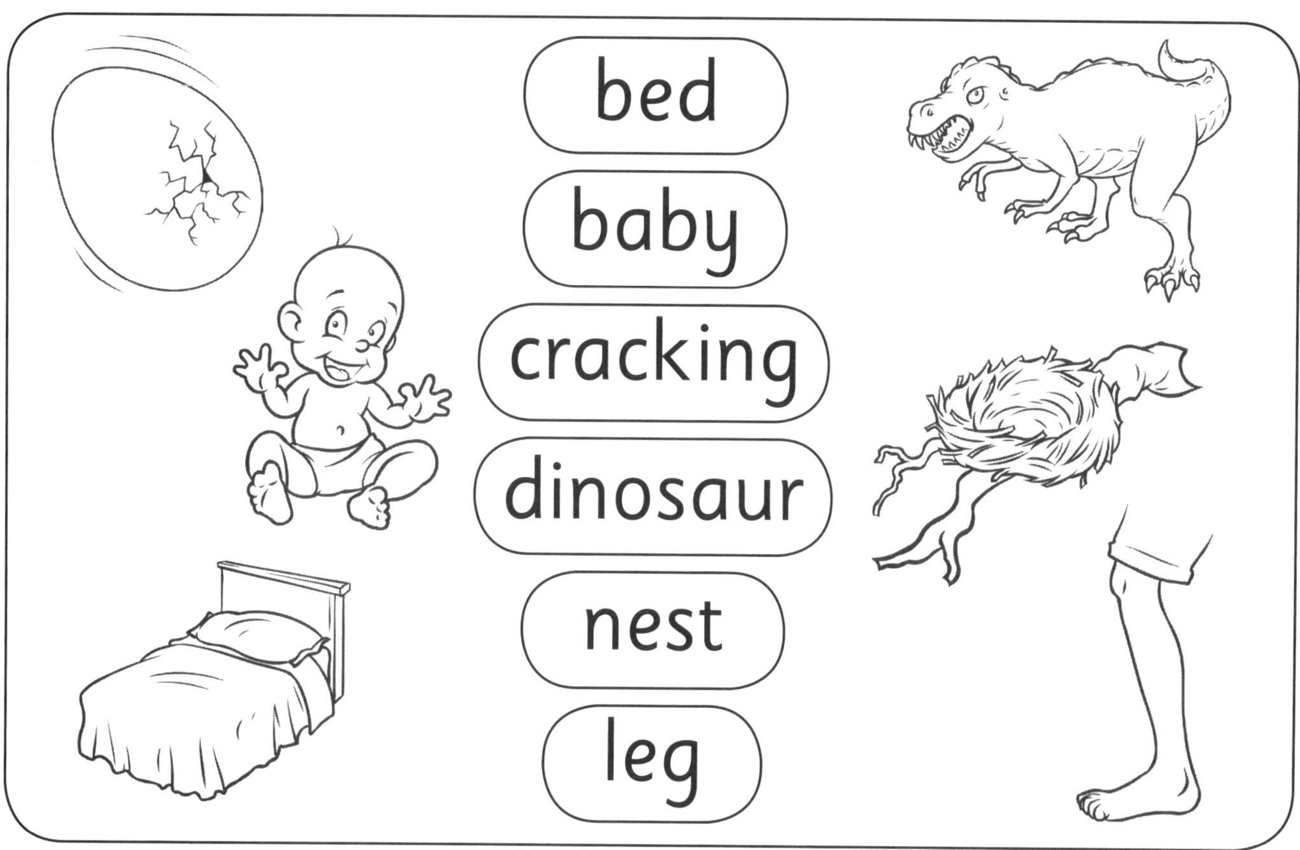

2 Find the words. Colour the **ing** words red, **ed** words blue and **eg** words green.

b	r	e	a	k	i	n	g	a	j	k	e
d	o	i	n	g	r	o	l	l	i	n	g
m	q	c	r	a	c	k	i	n	g	a	e
u	p	e	g	e	g	g	l	e	g	b	i
f	p	l	e	d	p	v	b	e	d	x	y
r	e	d	h	s	g	r	c	y	w	e	d

Lesson 73 the sounds **et** and **ed**

Learning objectives

Children will:

- read and write et and ed words.
- recognise the days of the week.

Australian Curriculum Content Descriptions

Sound and letter knowledge

ACELA1439 listen to the sounds a student hears in the word, and write letters to represent those sounds; identify and manipulate sounds (phonemes) in spoken words

ACELA1440 identify familiar and recurring letters and the use of upper and lower case in written texts

Expressing and developing ideas

ACELA1435 learn that word order in sentences is important for meaning

ACELA1438 build word families using onset and rime

ACELA1758 recognise the most common sound made by each letter of the alphabet, including consonants and short vowel sounds; write consonant-vowel-consonant words by writing letters to represent the sounds in the spoken words; know that spoken words are written down by listening to the sounds heard in the word and then writing letters to represent those sounds

Word families

fed, bed, led, ted, red, wed, pet, net, jet, vet, wet, hen, ten, pen, leg, egg

Vocabulary words

Monday, Tuesday, Wednesday, Thursday, Friday, Saturday, Sunday

Extra assistance

The days of the week should be learnt as a set of sight words, but also as a concept. Days of the week are often visualised as a discrete set, but it is important to give students the concept of them as a cycle. One way to reinforce this is to make a circular weekly chart. Put the activities that repeat each week on the chart and refer to it each morning. Turn the chart to show today and talk about the name of the day and what happens: Today is Tuesday (point and spell the word). On Tuesdays we always go to the library after lunch.

Classroom activities

Mind the Gap!

Write these sentences on the board:

On ____ Meg lays ten eggs.

On ____ Meg has a rest.

Give students flashcards with the days of the week on them. Ask them to hold up the card showing each day, then fill the gaps. Give the students a set of similar sentences to write out and fill in themselves. Discuss their answers.

Reading Eggs Lesson sequence	TEACH Content and skills	PRACTISE Children will:	APPLY
Hear: *Animated Lesson*	Introduce the sound *et* through the song *Sid thinks et.*	sort the *et* and *ed* words and match to pictures.	**Worksheet 1** Word families
Write: *Look, Listen and Spell, Make a Sentence*	Identify sounds in a word and write the word. Recognise correct word order for a sentence.	sound out a word and select letters to spell it correctly. Choose the correct words to make a sentence.	**Worksheet 2** Read and write
Find: *Word Family, Alphabet Foods, Missing Sound, Golden Goose, Frog Logs*	Identify the correct onset letter to complete the word. Identify initial letters. Recognise a given word.	choose the correct initial letter to make the word. Match pictures to their initial letter. Find the given word in a group.	**Worksheet 3** Vocabulary
Vocabulary: *Word Windows, Today's Words*	Build vocabulary skills: Blend and recognise words. Recognise key vocabulary.	blend sounds to read words. Tap on the word being said.	**Worksheet 4** Check
Read: *Book Ends, Picture Picker, Book*	Read sentences using basic vocabulary. Read aloud book.	choose from a list of words to finish the sentence. Read a sentence and match to a picture. Listen, follow the reading and read along.	**Reading Eggs Story book** Meg the hen

Classroom activities

Find the Sound

Give each student a card with the sound *et* on one side and *ed* on the other. Say a word and ask students to listen to the end sound. They should hold up the card to show that sound. Use clear, recognisable words such as: get, bed, met, fed.

Related Reading Eggs Activities, Interactives, Songs and Books

Driving Tests

Test 5

Sight words: get

Letters and sounds: vet

Content words: Monday, Tuesday, Wednesday, Thursday, Friday, Saturday, Sunday

Spelling Bank

Music Café

Sid thinks et

Jazz thinks ed

Reading Eggs Puzzle Park

Hidden Words

Song Lines

What is it?

Fingers

Reading Eggs Posters

Reading Eggs Library Books

My Program Books

Critter Card

Meg the hen

Teacher Toolkit

Spelling Activities

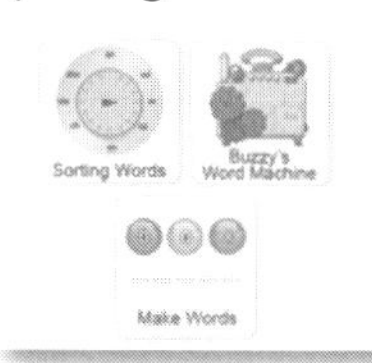

Reading Eggs Apps

Eggy Sight words

Eggy Snap

Eggy Phonics 1

et ed

Lesson 73 · Worksheet 1

Name

Word families

1 Use the word wheel to make a list of **et** words.

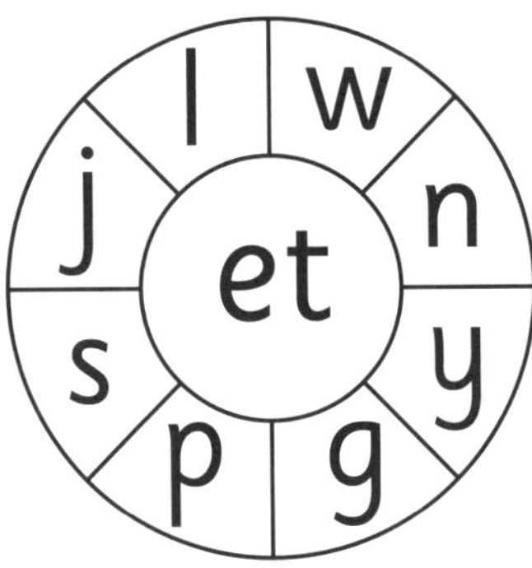

2 Circle the rhyming words in each row.

egg	met	leg	red	beg
fed	jet	peg	bet	vet
bed	wed	pet	led	ten

3 Colour the end sound.

Name

Read and write

Lesson 73 • Worksheet 2

1 Match each sentence to a picture.

On Monday,
Meg the hen lays ten eggs.

On Tuesday,
Meg looks at a book.

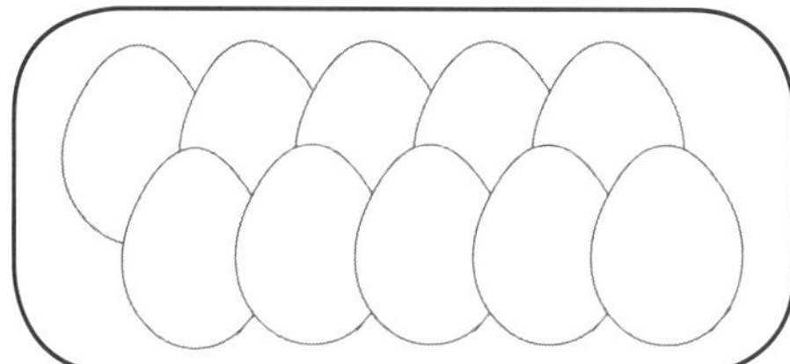

On Wednesday,
Meg gets ten little, red beds.

On Thursday,
Meg gets ten red pens.

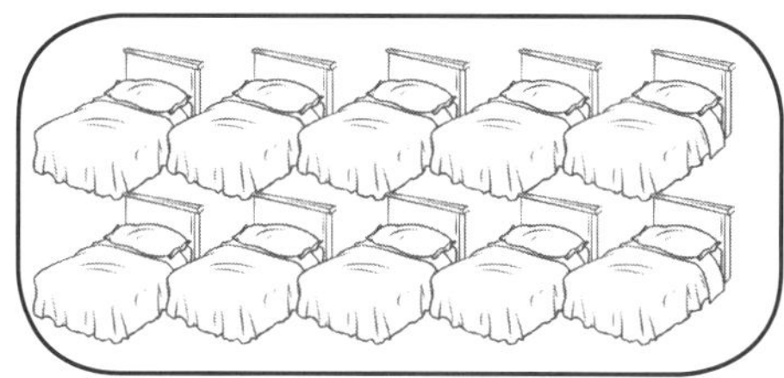

On Friday,
Meg gets ten little bells.

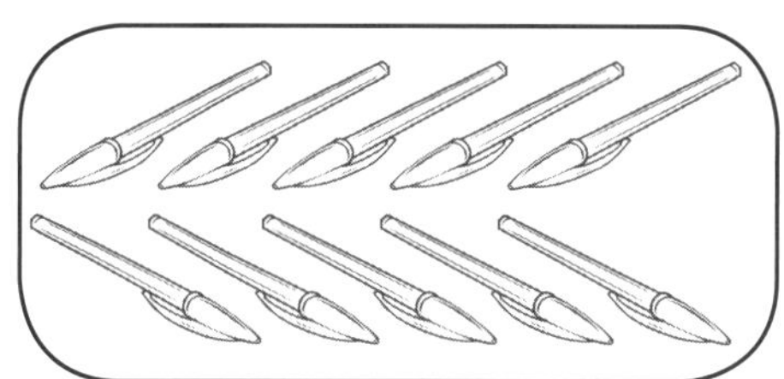

2 Finish these sentences.

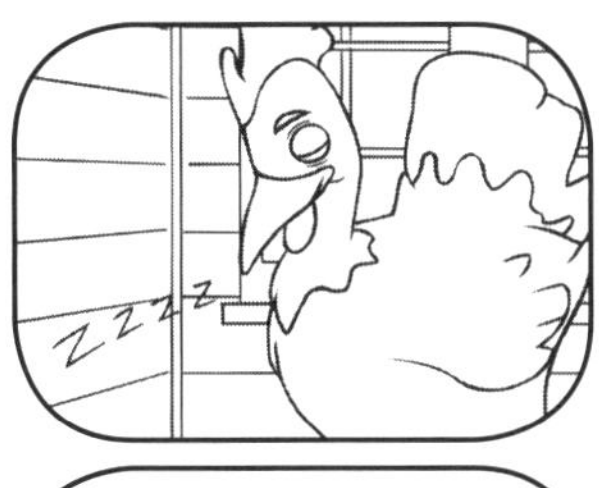

On Saturday, ______________________

______________________________.

On Sunday, ______________________

______________________________.

Vocabulary

Lesson 73 · Worksheet 3

Name

1 Find the matching pairs.

Wednesday	Sunday	Tuesday
Tuesday	Monday	Wednesday
Friday	Thursday	Sunday
Monday	Friday	Saturday
Saturday		Thursday

2 Put the days of the week in order.

Saturday ____________________

Tuesday ____________________

Monday ____________________

Sunday ____________________

Thursday ____________________

Wednesday ____________________

Friday ____________________

Name

Check

Lesson 73 • Worksheet 4

1 Join each word to a picture.

2 How many sounds do you hear in each word? Colour the box.

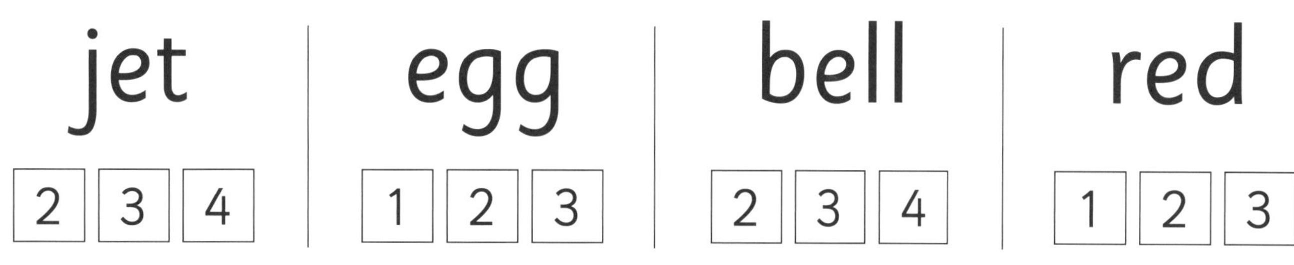

3 Write each word in the matching boxes.

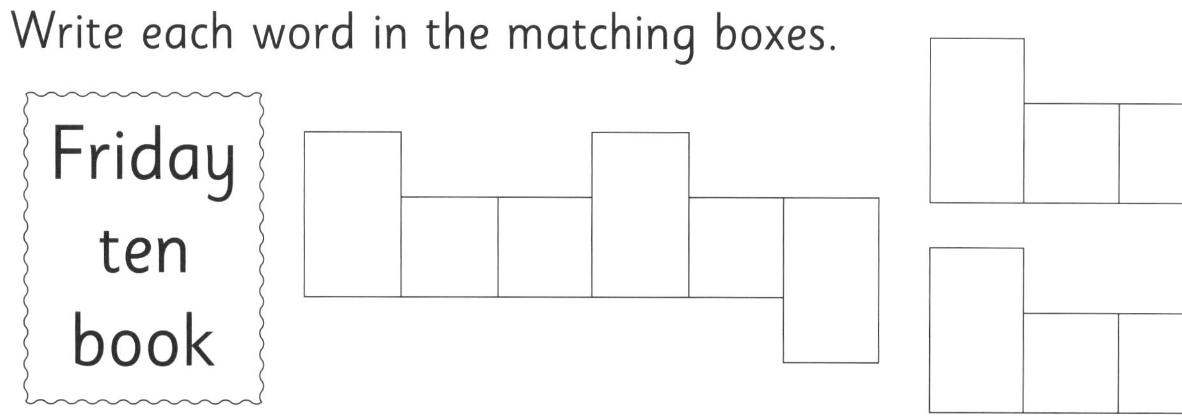

Lesson 74 the sounds **eg** and **et**

Learning objectives

Children will:

- read and write eg and et words.
- recognise words for pets.

Australian Curriculum Content Descriptions

Sound and letter knowledge

ACELA1439 listen to the sounds a student hears in the word, and write letters to represent those sounds; identify rhyme and syllables in spoken words; identify and manipulate sounds (phonemes) in spoken words

Creating texts

ACELY1653 follow clear demonstrations of how to construct each letter, learn to construct lower case letters

Expressing and developing ideas

ACELA1435 learn that word order in sentences is important for meaning

ACELA1438 build word families using onset and rime

ACELA1758 recognise the most common sound made by each letter of the alphabet, including consonants and short vowel sounds; write consonant-vowel-consonant words by writing letters to represent the sounds in the spoken words; know that spoken words are written down by listening to the sounds heard in the word and then writing letters to represent those sounds

Word families

egg, leg, peg, pet, vet, net, wet

Vocabulary words

horse, bird, dog, fish, frog, cat, rabbit, mouse

Extra assistance

When making word family lists, teach students to run through the alphabet and try each letter as a starting sound to go with the rime. They need to look for the "real" words. For example:

leg meg ~~neg~~ peg

Can students think of any words starting with two or more letters? More advanced students may apply blends and common consonant pairings such as *st* and *dr*.

Classroom activities

Throw it Away!

Sit in a circle with a box in the middle. Students each hold two or more items, pictures or words on cards. They take turns telling what their item, picture or word is. If the object ends with *eg* or *et* or *ed* they throw it into the box. Discuss the objects with the class.

Mind the Gap!

Write this sentence on the board: My pet is a ____ . Read the sentence together and brainstorm a list of possible answers. Students should copy the sentence into their book and finish it with their choice of word and matching illustration.

Reading Eggs Lesson sequence	**TEACH Content and skills**	**PRACTISE Children will:**	**APPLY**
Hear: *Animated Lesson*	Introduce the sound *eg* through the song *Meg thinks eg.*	identify the *eg* sound.	**Worksheet 1** Word families
Write: *Dot-to-dot, Pick Up Bricks*	Reinforce correct letter formation. Recognise correct word order for a sentence.	write the word *egg*. Choose the correct words to make a sentence.	**Worksheet 2** Read and write
Find: *Word Family*	Identify the correct onset letter to complete the word.	choose the correct initial letter to make the word.	**Worksheet 3** Vocabulary
Vocabulary: *Groups, The Theme Game, Blend a Word, Rhyming Squares, Word Dominoes, Break it Up, Power Words*	Build vocabulary skills: Recognise categories of words. Recognise key vocabulary. Blend and recognise words. Identify rhyming words. Identify the number of phonemes in a word.	match pictures to categories. Match pictures to words. Blend sounds to read words. Find images of rhyming words. Identify the number of sounds in a word.	**Worksheet 4** Check
Read: *How Does it End?, Book*	Read sentences using basic vocabulary. Read aloud book.	read a beginning and match it to the correct ending. Listen, follow the reading and read along.	**Reading Eggs nonfiction book** Pets

Related Reading Eggs Activities, Interactives, Songs and Books

Driving Tests

Spelling Bank

Music Café

Meg thinks eg

Reading Eggs Puzzle Park

Hidden Words
Song Lines
Animal Fun
What is it?

Reading Eggs Posters

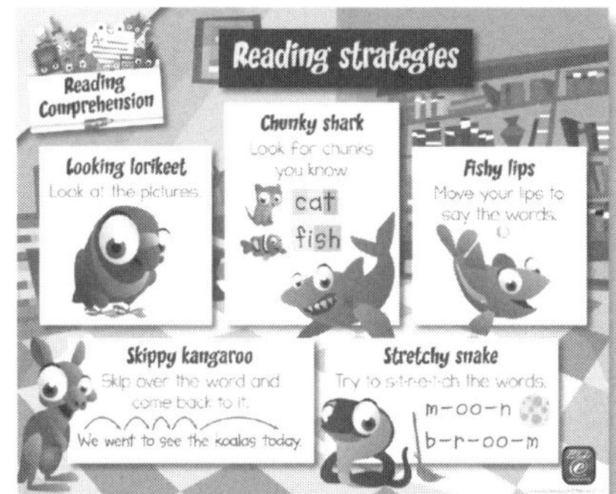

Reading Eggs Library Books

My Program Books

Critter Card

Red rooster

Teacher Toolkit

Spelling Activities

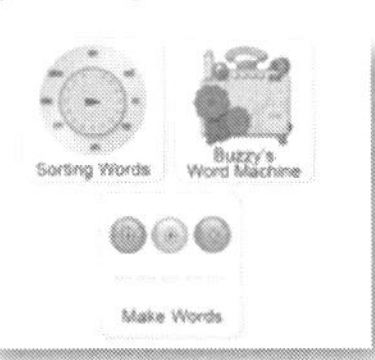

Reading Eggs Apps

Eggy Sight words

Eggy Phonics 1

eg et

Lesson 74 • Worksheet 1

Name

Word families

1 Make a word with each letter using **eg** or **et**.

l________ m________ g________

p________ b________ v________

j________ n________ w________

2 Label the pictures.

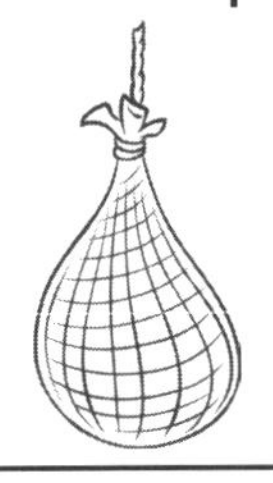

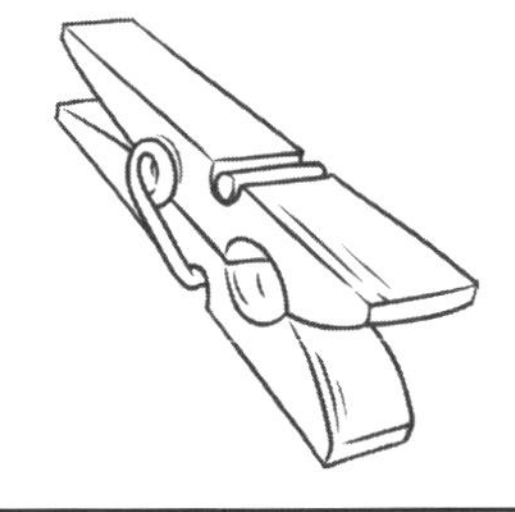

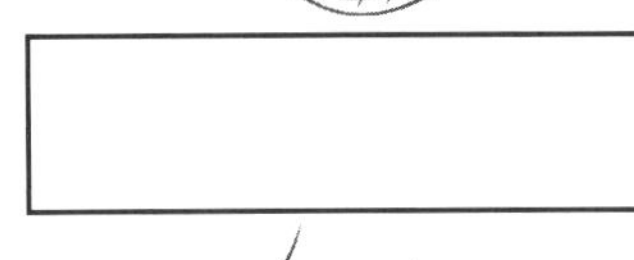

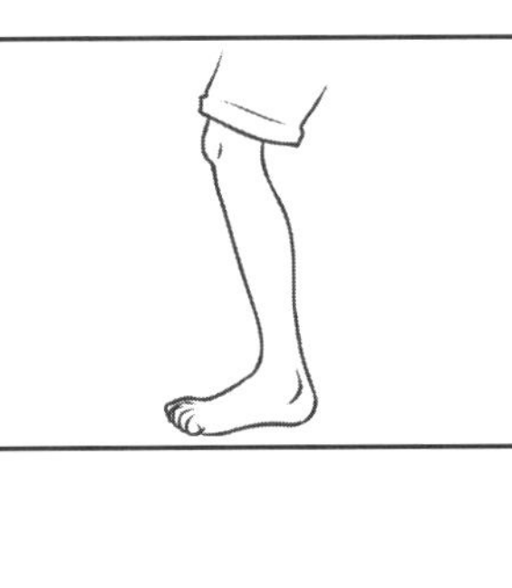

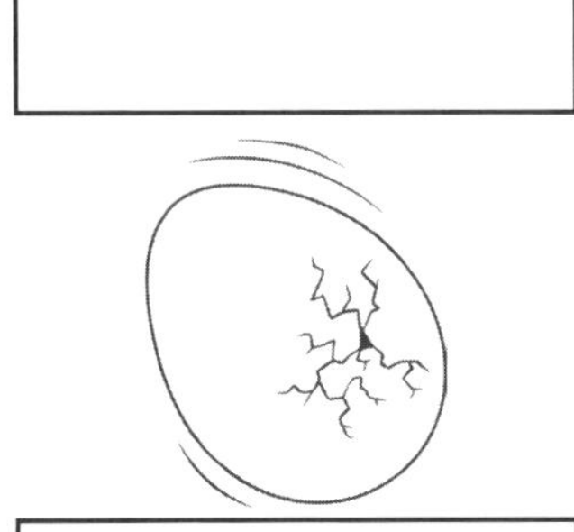

3 Circle the rhyming words in each row.

cog leg sag peg leg

net sat met but vet

Name

Read and write

Lesson 74 • Worksheet 2

Finish the sentences.

cat dog frog rabbit

My pet is a

_______________.

My pet is a

_______________.

My pet is a

_______________.

My pet is a

_______________.

Vocabulary

Lesson 74 · Worksheet 3

Name

1 Label each pet with the correct word.

cat	bird	dog
fish	mouse	horse
rabbit		frog

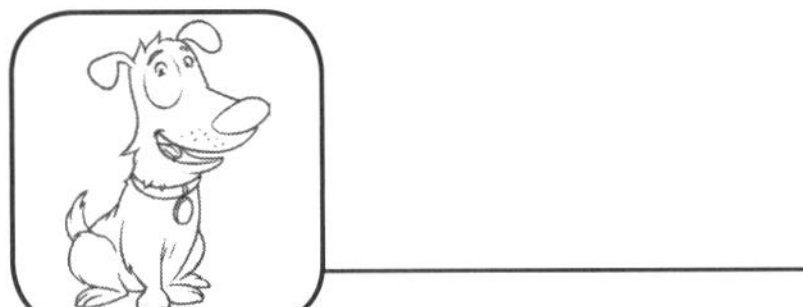

2 Finish this sentence.

My pet is a ______________________.

Name

Check

Lesson 74 • Worksheet 4

1 Colour the **end** sound.

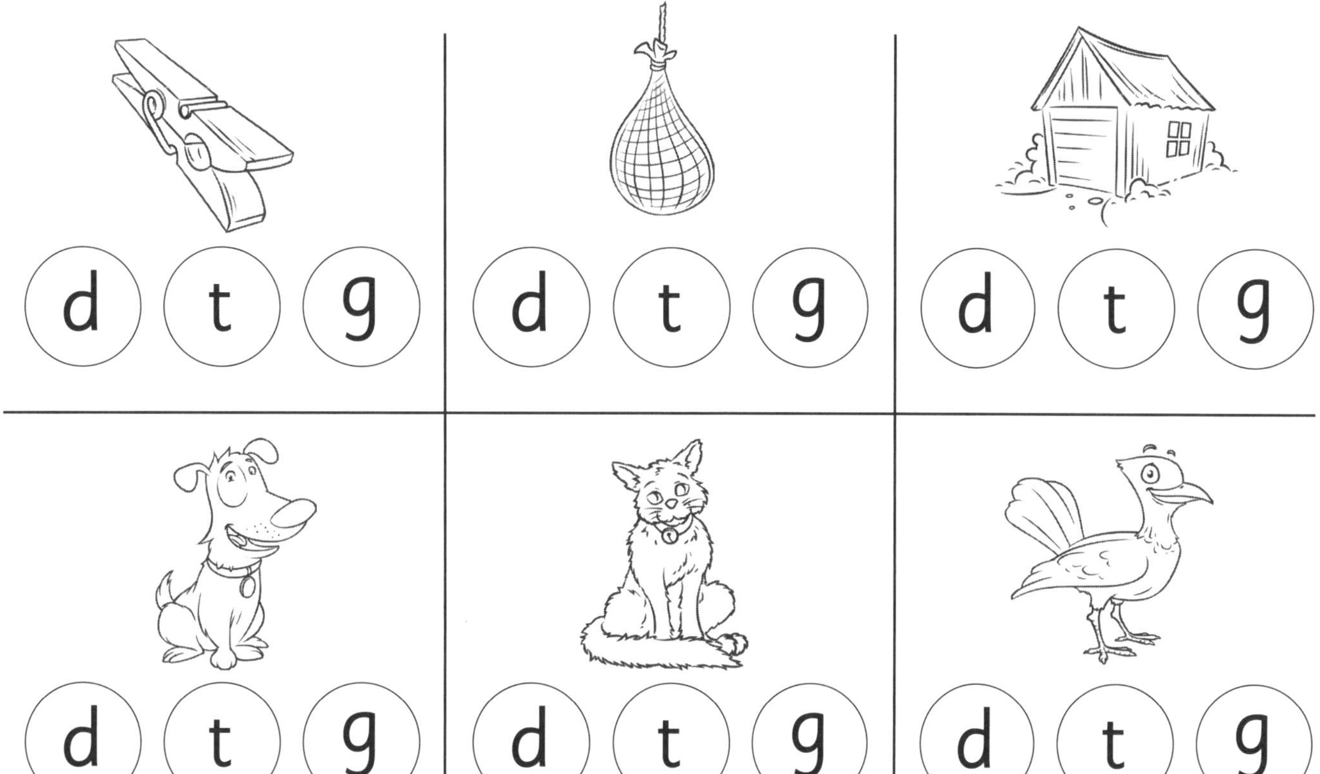

2 Crack the code!

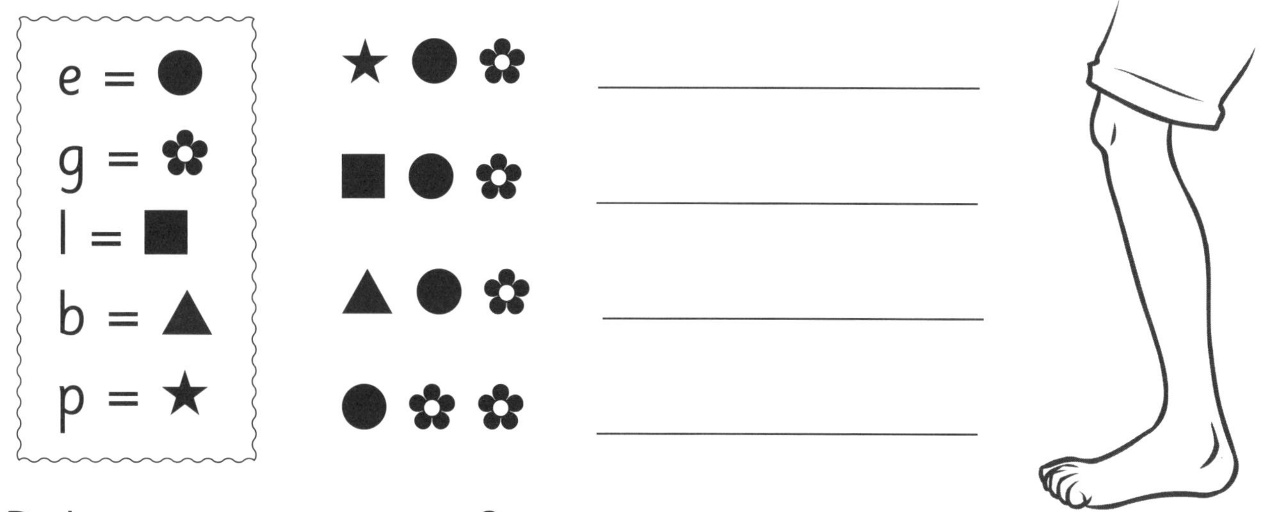

Did you spot a pattern?

Lesson 75 the word **where**, the sound **en**

Learning objectives

Children will:

- identify and read the words where and when.
- read and write en words.

Australian Curriculum Content Descriptions

Sound and letter knowledge

ACELA1439 listen to the sounds a student hears in the word, and write letters to represent those sounds; identify rhyme and syllables in spoken words; identify and manipulate sounds (phonemes) in spoken words

Expressing and developing ideas

ACELA1435 learn that word order in sentences is important for meaning

ACELA1437 build vocabulary through multiple speaking and listening experiences

ACELA1438 build word families using onset and rime

ACELA1758 recognise the most common sound made by each letter of the alphabet, including consonants and short vowel sounds; write consonant-vowel-consonant words by writing letters to represent the sounds in the spoken words; know that spoken words are written down by listening to the sounds heard in the word and then writing letters to represent those sounds

Sight words

where, when, now, up, down

Word families

ten, pen, men, hen, when

Vocabulary words

ladder, climb

Extra assistance

Making a list of question starters (such as *where* and *when*) and putting it up in the classroom can help students feel more confident about participating in class discussions. Clues as to how to ask questions and what question to ask will give students a prompt for asking their own questions. Direct the class to these prompts during discussions of written, visual and audible texts, such as books, video clips, speeches and observations of items.

Classroom activities

Word Wheel

Give each student two circles of cardboard, one larger than the other, joined through the centre with a split pin. On the visible edge of the larger circle write the consonant letters *b, l, m, p, t, w*. On the smaller circle write the rimes *et, ed, eg, en*, so they will match up with the outer letters and make words. Have students turn the circles and write out the words they make.

Answer Your Own Question!

On the board write the question: Where are you going? Read the question together and brainstorm a list of possible answers. Ask students to write the question in their book and write an answer that is a full sentence; for example, I am going to school.

Reading Eggs Lesson sequence	TEACH Content and skills	PRACTISE Children will:	APPLY
Hear: *Animated Lesson*	Introduce the word *where*. Introduce the sound *en* through the song *Meg the hen thinks en*.	identify and read the word *where* in isolation and in a sentence. Identify the *en* sound.	**Worksheet 1** Word families
Write: *Make a Sentence*	Recognise correct word order for a sentence.	choose the correct words to make a sentence.	**Worksheet 2** Read and write
Find: *Word Family, Buzzy's Word Machine, Missing Sound, Squirter, Shooting Stars, Time for 20*	Identify the correct onset letter to complete the word. Identify word endings. Recognise a given word.	choose the correct initial letter to make the word. Match the word to its ending. Find the given word in a group.	**Worksheet 3** Sight words
Vocabulary: *Blend a Word, Word Whiz, Today's Words, Rhyme Time*	Build vocabulary skills: Blend and recognise words. Recognise key vocabulary. Identify rhyming words.	blend sounds to read words. Tap on the word being said and put it in a sentence. Find images of rhyming words.	**Worksheet 4** Check
Read: *Book*	Read aloud book.	listen, follow the reading and read along.	**Reading Eggs Story book** The slide

Related Reading Eggs Activities, Interactives, Songs and Books

Driving Tests

Map 1

Lesson 7

Focus sound words: ten, men, pen, wet, net, met, vet

High frequency sight words: get

Challenge: when

Spelling Bank

Music Café

Meg the hen thinks en

Reading Eggs Puzzle Park

Hidden Words

Song Lines

Arrows

Opposites

Reading Eggs Posters

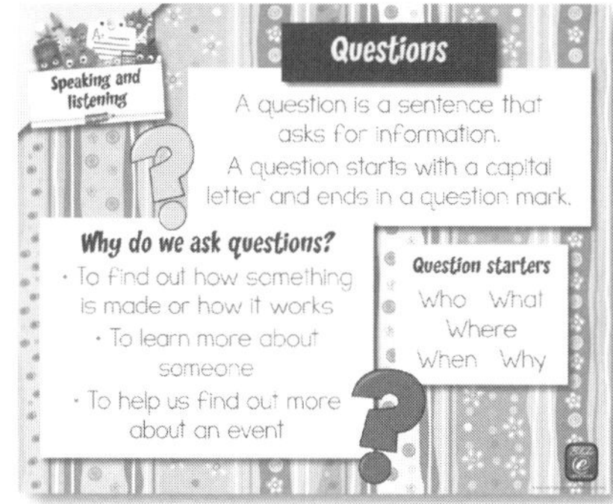

Reading Eggs Library Books

My Program Books

Critter Card

Jet set

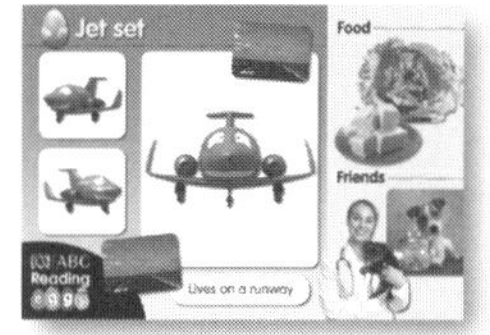

Teacher Toolkit

Spelling Activities

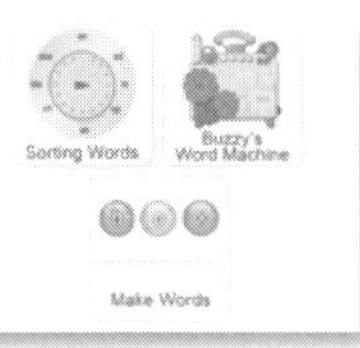

Reading Eggs Apps

Eggy Sight words

Eggy Snap

en

Name

Word families

Lesson 75 • Worksheet 1

1 Put the letters through the word machine. What words can you make?

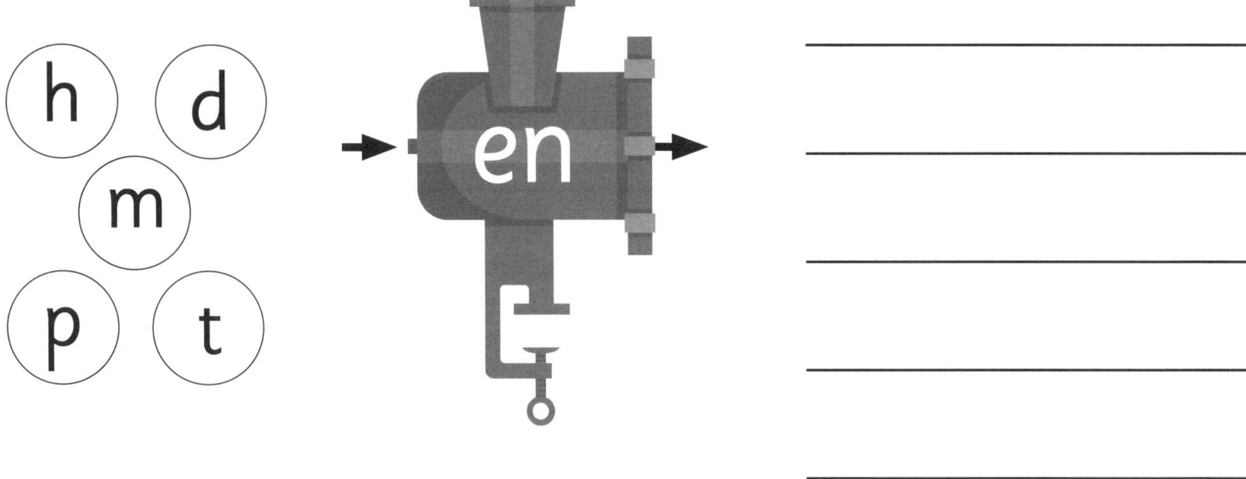

2 Draw ten men with a pen and a hen.

Name

Read and write

where

Lesson 75 • Worksheet 2

1 Add **ing** to these doing words.

climb__________ walk__________

look__________ talk__________

2 Put the words above in these sentences.

Sam is ____________ the ladder.

Jazz is ____________ away.

Sid is ____________ at the slide.

Meg is ____________ to Sam.

3 Join the question to the correct answer.

Where is Sam?	at the slide
Where is Sid?	on the ladder

where

Lesson 75 • Worksheet 3

Name

Sight words

1 Trace and copy.

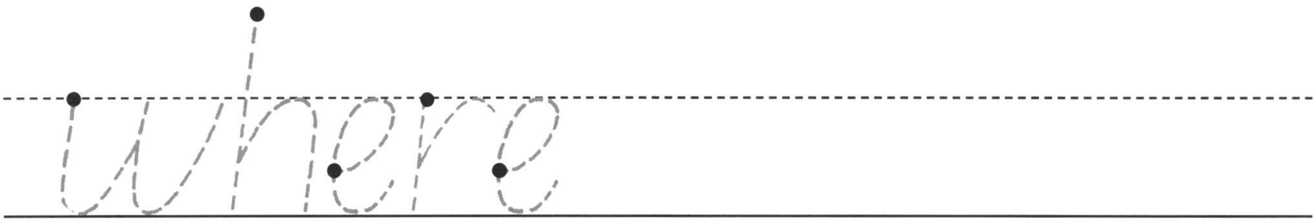

2 Match each sentence to a picture.

Where you can sleep.

Where you can play.

Where you can eat.

Where you can climb.

3 Finish the sentences using **Where** or **When**.

________________ are you coming?

________________ are you going?

Name

Check

Lesson 75 • Worksheet 4

1 Colour the correct word. Cross out the wrong word.

You go [up] [down] the ladder.

You go [up] [down] the slide.

2 Put the correct vowels in each word.

10 6 3 2

t___n s___x thr____ tw___

h___t sh___d b___nk sh___p

3 Which vowels are in your name?

____

Lesson 76 the sounds **en** and **eg**

Learning objectives

Children will:

- identify the rimes eg and en.
- read and write words from short e word families.

Australian Curriculum Content Descriptions

Sound and letter knowledge

ACELA1439 listen to the sounds a student hears in the word, and write letters to represent those sounds; identify and manipulate sounds (phonemes) in spoken words

Expressing and developing ideas

ACELA1435 learn that word order in sentences is important for meaning

ACELA1438 build word families using onset and rime

ACELA1758 write consonant-vowel-consonant words by writing letters to represent the sounds in the spoken words; know that spoken words are written down by listening to the sounds heard in the word and then writing letters to represent those sounds

Interpreting, analysing and evaluating

ACELY1649 navigate a text correctly, starting at the right place and reading in the right direction, returning to the next line as needed, matching one spoken word to one written word

Word families

peg, beg, egg, leg, Meg, ten, hen, men, pen, Ben, peck, net, get, wet, set, jet, red, fed, bed, Ned

Vocabulary words

eyes, nose, spotty, purple, yellow, orange, pink

Extra assistance

Some languages do not distinguish between long and short vowels, Korean has no short /e/ sound, so these words may be difficult for some students to pronounce. Play word games that rely on correct pronunciation, such as Go Fish with flashcards of short *a, e, i, o* and *u* words. Play Bingo with these words as it relies on distinguishing the vowel sounds aurally.

Classroom activities

Run to it!

This is best done in a large room with furniture pushed out of the way, or on the playground. Label 4 corners or areas with signs saying *et, en, ed* and *eg*. The students stand in the middle and when the teacher calls out a word containing one of these sounds, they must run to the matching corner.
Try harder words, with more than one syllable, for example: letter, given and bedroom.

Word Pairs

Give half the class a consonant on a card. Give the other half of the class a short e rime on a card. Ask the children to find a partner to make a word and sit together. Ask each consonant person to write their word on the board. Have the pairs swap cards and play again – they must make a different word this time!

Reading Eggs Lesson sequence	TEACH Content and skills	PRACTISE Children will:	APPLY
Hear: *Animated Lesson*	Identify the word families *en* and *eg*.	sort the *en* and *eg* words, and match to pictures.	**Worksheet 1** Word families
Write: *Pick Up Bricks*	Recognise correct word order for a sentence.	choose the correct words to make a sentence.	**Worksheet 2** Read and write
Find: *Word Family, Word Sort, Jumping Astronauts, Gronk, Read and Colour*	Identify the correct onset letter to complete the word. Identify starting and ending sounds. Recognise a given word. Identify colour words.	choose the correct initial letter to make the word. Sort words into boxes for start or end sounds. Find the given word in a group. Use correct colours.	**Worksheet 3** Vocabulary
Vocabulary: *Word Windows, Tiles, Words per Minute*	Build vocabulary skills: Blend and recognise words. Recognise key vocabulary.	blend sounds to read and make words. Match pictures to words.	**Worksheet 4** Check
Read: *Book Ends, Bubble Popper, Book*	Read sentences using basic vocabulary. Read aloud book.	choose a word to finish the sentence. Read and follow instructions. Listen, follow the reading and read along.	**Reading Eggs Story book** Eggs on legs

Related Reading Eggs Activities, Interactives, Songs and Books

Spelling Bank

Ants

Lesson 6

Focus sound words: bed, red, fed, wed, peg, beg, legs

Challenge: shed, egg

Driving Tests

Music Café

Meg the hen thinks eg

Meg the hen thinks en

Reading Eggs Puzzle Park

Colour Code

Animal Colours

Number Nuts

Teddy Bear

Reading Eggs Posters

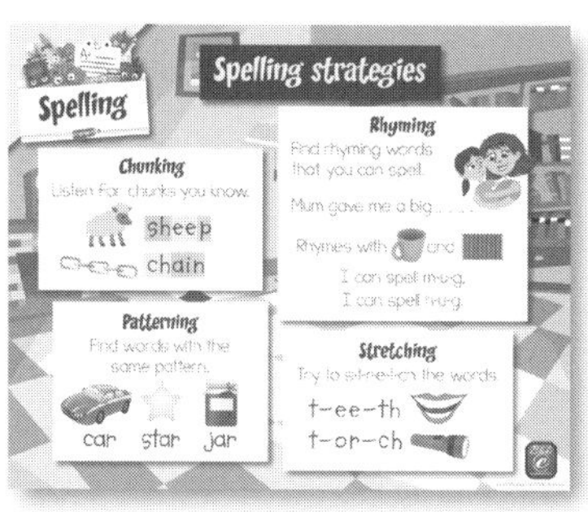

Reading Eggs Library Books

My Program Books

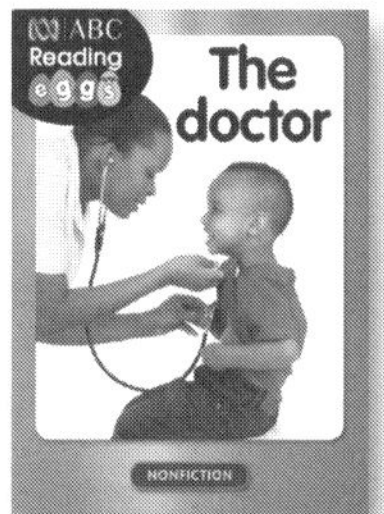

Critter Card

Peggy leg

Teacher Toolkit

Spelling Activities

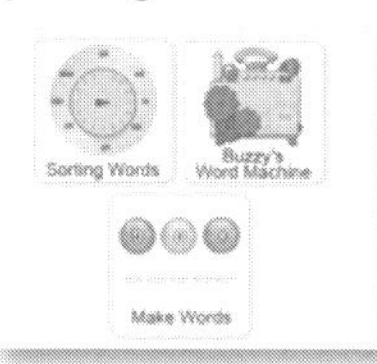

Reading Eggs Apps

Eggy Sight words

Eggy Snap

en eg

Lesson 76 • Worksheet 1

Name

Word families

1 Use the word wheels to make words.

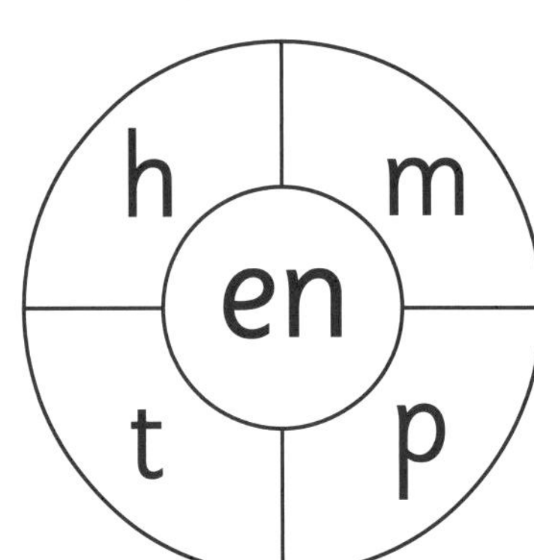

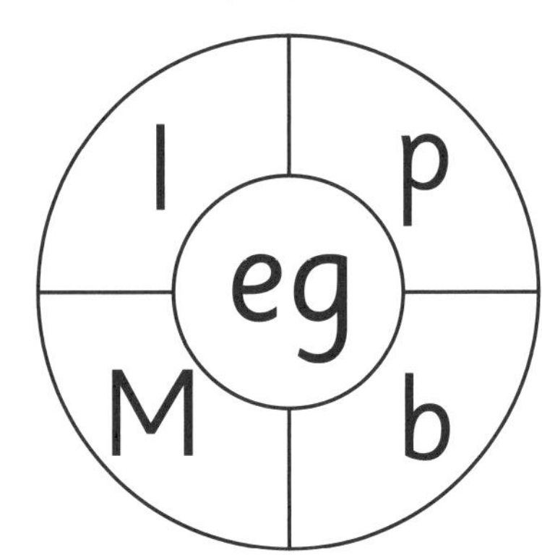

2 Join each word to a picture.

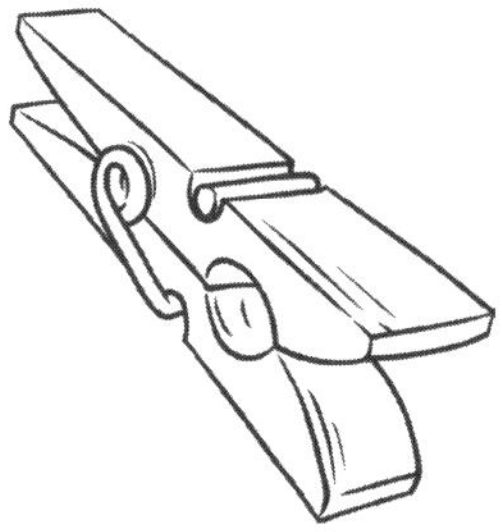

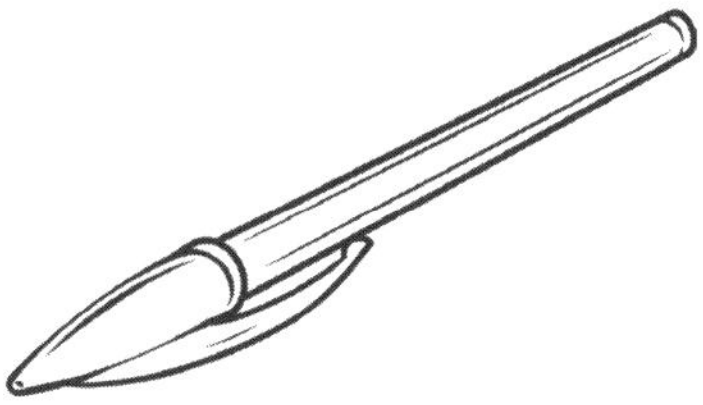

pen

egg

peg

hen

leg

ten

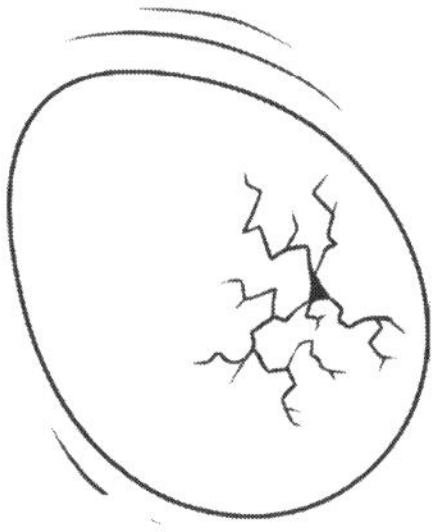

Name

Read and write

Lesson 76 • Worksheet 2

Put the words in order to make each sentence.

fed. The eggs on legs get

eggs get legs wet. The on

bed. into eggs The get on legs

egg legs. gets Ned red a on

Vocabulary

Lesson 76 · Worksheet 3

Name

Read the instructions to colour the pictures.

Her hair is brown.

Put purple spots on her top.

The girl has blue eyes.

The boy has green eyes.

His hair is black.

Put yellow dots on his top.

Name

Check

en eg

Lesson 76 • Worksheet 4

1 Write each word.

2 Colour the words for the colours.

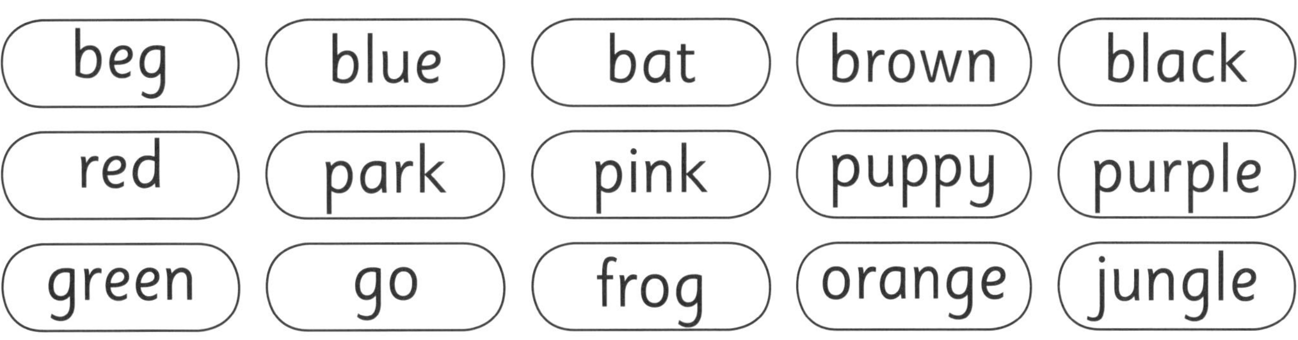

3 Write as many words as you can that rhyme with **pen**.

Lesson 77 the words **who** and **lives**

Learning objectives

Children will:

- identify and read the words who, lives and here.
- read and write animal words.

Australian Curriculum Content Descriptions

Sound and letter knowledge

ACELA1439 listen to the sounds a student hears in the word, and write letters to represent those sounds; identify rhyme and syllables in spoken words; identify and manipulate sounds (phonemes) in spoken words

Expressing and developing ideas

ACELA1434 explore spoken, written and multimodal texts and identify elements, for example words and images

ACELA1435 learn that word order in sentences is important for meaning

ACELA1437 build vocabulary through multiple speaking and listening experiences

ACELA1758 recognise the most common sound made by each letter of the alphabet, including consonants and short vowel sounds; write consonant-vowel-consonant words by writing letters to represent the sounds in the spoken words; know that spoken words are written down by listening to the sounds heard in the word and then writing letters to represent those sounds

Sight words

who, here

Vocabulary words

elephant, butterfly, dolphin, monkey, zebra, bird, lives, tiger, giraffe, fly, jungle, sea

Extra assistance

Writing and answering questions is an important skill in many school subjects. Give students opportunities to practise writing questions and also writing answers.

A question is a sentence that asks for information: who, when, where, why, what is it, how many, what colour or shape, how long, and so on. A question starts with a capital letter and ends with a question mark.

Ideally, a question should be answered with a sentence which repeats part of the question. For example: Where does a dolphin live? A dolphin lives in the sea.

Classroom activities

Sentence Shuffle

Write and jumble an enlarged version of the sentence: Dolphins can swim in the sea. Read it with the children and ask them to work out the correct order. Reproduce the sentence on small cards so students can make the sentence themselves and read it. Suggest clues such as capital letters and full stops. Discuss the sentence when they are done.

Reading Eggs Lesson sequence	**TEACH Content and skills**	**PRACTISE Children will:**	**APPLY**
Write: *Dot-to-dot, Sound Streamers, Make a Sentence*	Reinforce correct letter formation. Identify sounds in words. Recognise correct word order for a sentence.	write the word *who*. Sound out and make words. Choose the correct words to make a sentence.	**Worksheet 1** Read and write
Find: *Jumping Astronauts, Squirter*	Recognise a given word.	find the given word in a group.	**Worksheet 2** Sight words
Match: *Rhyming Squares, Shooting Stars*	Identify rhyming words. Recognise a given word.	find images of rhyming words. Match the words which are the same.	**Worksheet 3** Vocabulary
Vocabulary: *The Theme Game, Word Whiz, City Zoo, Break it Up*	Build vocabulary skills: Recognise key vocabulary. Identify the number of phonemes in a word.	match pictures to written and verbal words. Put words in sentences. Identify the number of sounds in a word.	**Worksheet 4** Check
Read: *How Does it End?, Book*	Read sentences using basic vocabulary. Read aloud book.	read a beginning and match it to an ending. Listen, follow the reading and read along.	**Reading Eggs nonfiction** Who lives here?

Classroom activities

Bingo!

Give students a laminated board with ten squares on it. Ask them to write an animal word in each square from a list of 15 or more animals (use whiteboard markers). Hold up images of animals from the list. Students put a cross on that word on their board. First one to ten calls out 'bingo' and wins!

Related Reading Eggs Activities, Interactives, Songs and Books

Driving Tests

Test 4

Sight words: who, lives, here

Spelling Bank

Reading Eggs Puzzle Park

More than One

Animal Fun

Fingers

Do You Know?

Reading Eggs Posters

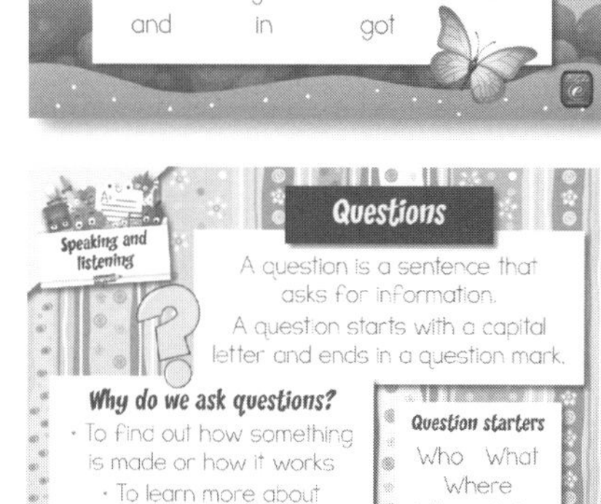

Reading Eggs Library Books

My Program Books

Critter Card

Big Ben

Teacher Toolkit

Spelling Activities

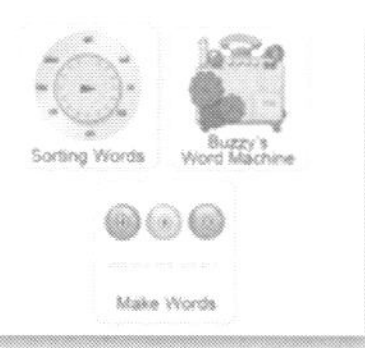

Grammar Lessons

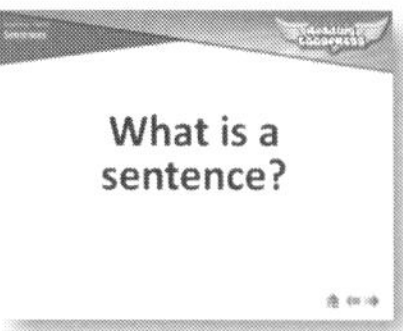

Reading Eggs Apps

Eggy Sight words

Eggy Snap

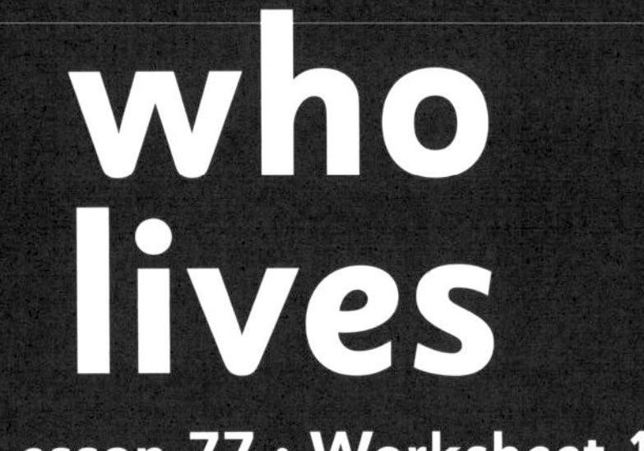

Name

Read and write

Who lives here? Complete the answers.

A __________ lives here.

cat bird fish

A __________ lives here.

cat bird fish

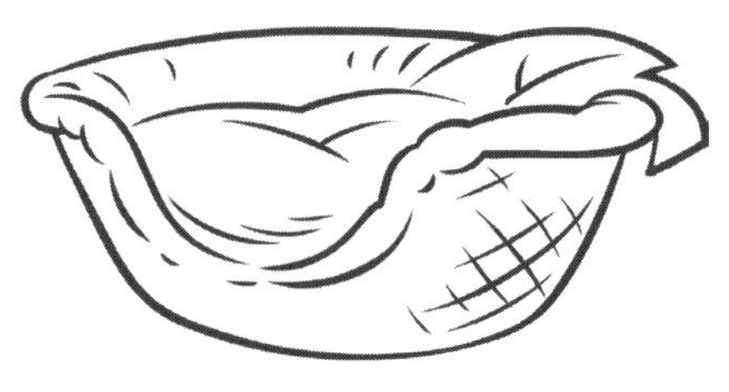

A __________ lives here.

duck dog dolphin

A __________ lives here.

duck dog dolphin

Name

Sight words

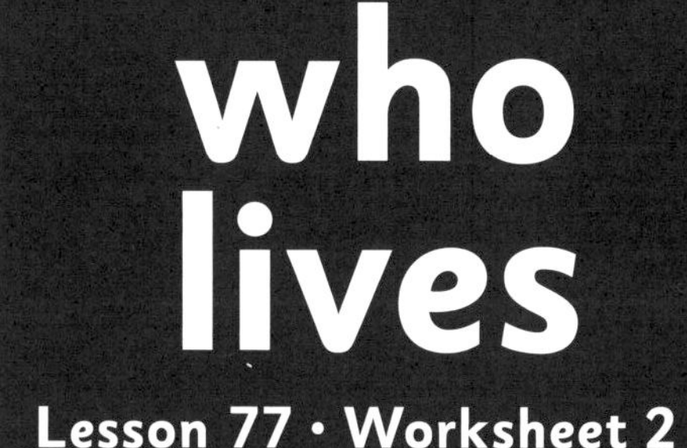

1 Trace and write the words.

Who lives here?

2 Use the words above to complete the sentences.

_________ lives in a nest?

A bird _________ in a nest.

Birds live _________ .

3 Guess the word by its shape. Write each word in the boxes.

here who lives

Vocabulary

Lesson 77 • Worksheet 3

Name

Who lives here? Match the animal picture to its name and then to its home.

bird

dolphin

monkey

butterfly

turtle

fish

elephant

tiger

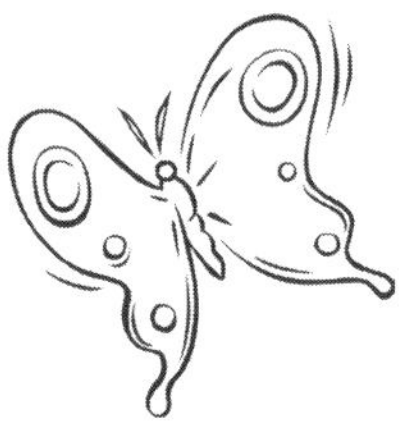

jungle

sea

tree

Name

Check

Lesson 77 • Worksheet 4

1 Label the pictures.

tree nest jungle sea

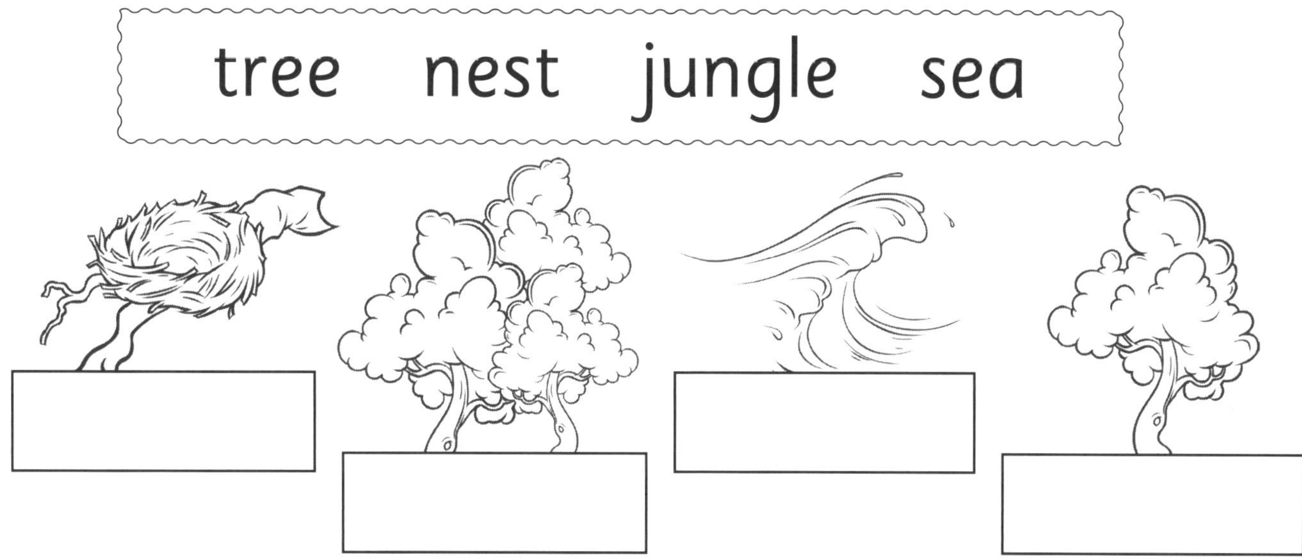

2 What can the animals do?

fly climb run swim

The monkey can ____________.

The dolphin can ____________.

The bird can ____________.

The zebra can ____________.

Lesson 78 the word **what**

Learning objectives

Children will:

- identify and read the word what.
- read and write words from a dragon theme.

Australian Curriculum Content Descriptions

Sound and letter knowledge

ACELA1439 listen to the sounds a student hears in the word, and write letters to represent those sounds; identify and manipulate sounds (phonemes) in spoken words

ACELA1440 identify familiar and recurring letters and the use of upper and lower case in written texts

Expressing and developing ideas

ACELA1435 learn that word order in sentences is important for meaning

ACELA1758 recognise the most common sound made by each letter of the alphabet, including consonants and short vowel sounds; know that spoken words are written down by listening to the sounds heard in the word and then writing letters to represent those sounds

Interpreting, analysing and evaluating

ACELY1649 navigate a text correctly, starting at the right place and reading in the right direction, returning to the next line as needed, matching one spoken word to one written word

Sight words

what

Vocabulary words

wings, tail, claws, fire, spikes, dragon, eye, lake, red, yellow, orange

Extra assistance

A strategy that can help independent readers is to look at the pictures for clues to work out unknown words. Sometimes knowing what sound it starts with and seeing the item or action in a picture is enough to help a child decipher the rest of the word. Most early reading books have quite literal pictures and sentences so using picture clues can be an easy way to decode unknown words.

Classroom activities

Make Your Own Questions

Put the question: What is in the lake? on the board. Read the question with the class and brainstorm a list of possible answers. Ask students to complete the question: What is in the __? with their own word. Then they swap with another student and write a full sentence answer. Discuss their questions and answers.

Reading Eggs Lesson sequence	TEACH Content and skills	PRACTISE Children will:	APPLY
Hear: *Animated Lesson*	Introduce the word *what.*	identify and read the word *what* in isolation and in a sentence.	**Worksheet 1** Sight words
Write: *Look, Listen and Spell, Make a Sentence*	Identify sounds in a word and write the word. Recognise correct word order for a sentence.	sound out a word and spell it correctly. Choose the correct words to make a sentence.	**Worksheet 2** Read and write
Find: *1, 2, 3, 4, Letter Lights, Hairy Heads, Missing Sound*	Identify the order of a sequence of events. Identify upper and lower case letters. Recognise a given word. Identify the correct onset letter to complete the word.	put pictures in order to show a sequence. Match lower case letters to their capital. Find the given word in a group. Choose the correct initial letter to make the word.	**Worksheet 3** Vocabulary
Vocabulary: *Make a Word, Word Windows, The Theme Game, Words per Minute*	Build vocabulary skills: Identify initial letters by sound and read written words. Blend and recognise words. Recognise key vocabulary.	match pictures to their initial letter. Match a word to its picture. Blend sounds to read words.	**Worksheet 4** Check
Read: *Book Ends, Book*	Read sentences using basic vocabulary. Read aloud book.	choose a word to finish the sentence. Listen, follow the reading and read along.	**Reading Eggs Story book** What is in the lake?

Classroom activities

Which Hat?

Place three hats on the floor with the labels *who, what* and *where*. Discuss the words. Students each hold an item, picture or word on a card. They take turns telling what their item, picture or word is. Then they must work out which hat it goes in – is it a person, an object or a place? Discuss their choice with the class.

Related Reading Eggs Activities, Interactives, Songs and Books

Driving Tests

Test 4

Sight words: what, who, lives, here

Spelling Bank

Reading Eggs Puzzle Park

More than One

Colour Code

What is it?

Finish the Alien

Reading Eggs Posters

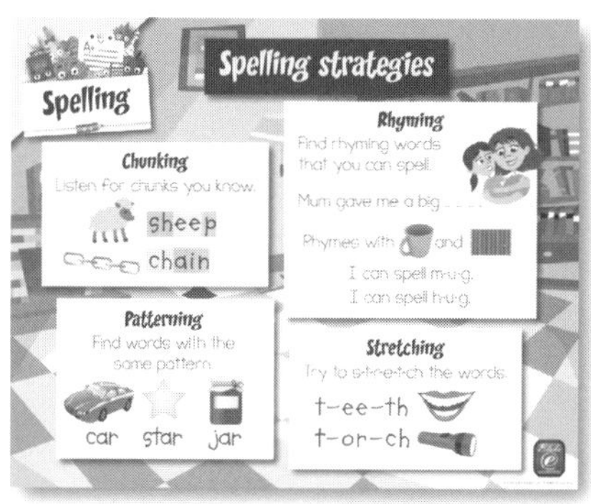

Reading Eggs Library Books

My Program Books

Critter Card

Wrecking ball

Teacher Toolkit

Spelling Activities

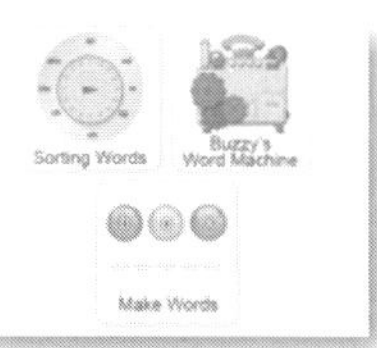

Reading Eggs Apps

Eggy Sight words

Eggy Snap

what

Lesson 78 • Worksheet 1

Name

Sight words

1 Trace and copy.

what

2 Finish the sentences with a word from the box.

What Who When Where

______ is that girl?

______ is the band playing?

______ is the party?

______ is in the lake?

Name

Read and write

Lesson 78 · Worksheet 2

1 Complete each sentence using words from the box. Draw a picture.

red	yellow	orange	fire	spikes	tail

I can see ______________

______________________.

I can ______________

______________________.

I ______________

______________________.

2 Colour each spike a colour that starts with that letter to make a pattern of dragon spikes.

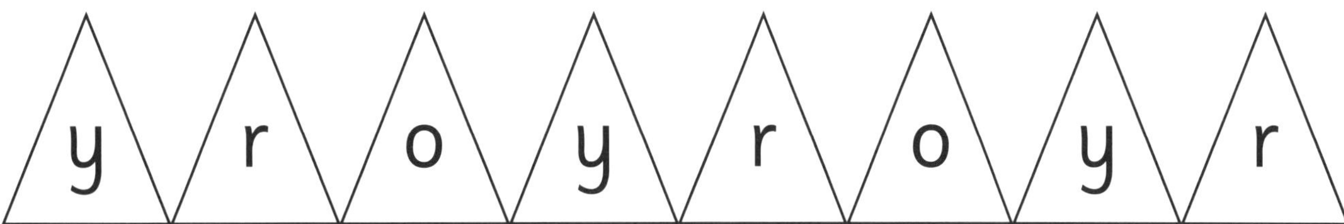

Vocabulary

Name

Lesson 78 • Worksheet 3

1 Join each word to a picture.

2 Colour the dragon to match the dragon in the book.

eyes = yellow
tail = red
wings = red
claws = yellow
spikes = yellow
dragon = red

Name

Check

Lesson 78 • Worksheet 4

1 Find the animal words and colour them.
dolphin = blue, dragon = red, butterfly = purple,
dinosaur = green, elephant = grey, monkey = orange

d	o	l	p	h	i	n	m	o	n	k	e	y
b	u	t	t	e	r	f	l	y	h	y	m	e
a	r	e	d	r	a	g	o	n	u	t	h	s
e	l	e	p	h	a	n	t	e	s	a	i	d
y	o	u	d	i	n	o	s	a	u	r	m	e

2 What is it? Label the pictures.

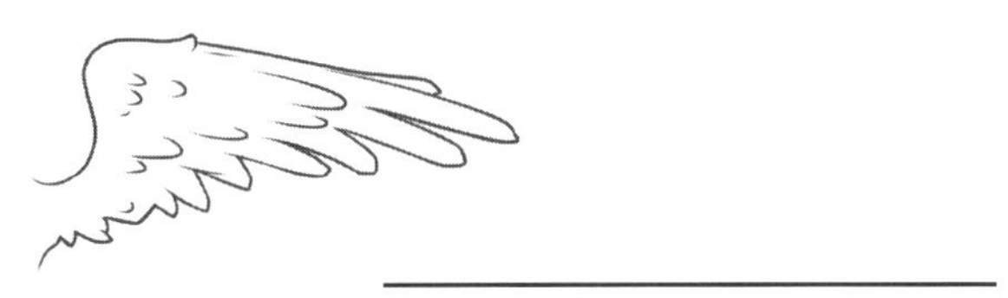

____

____

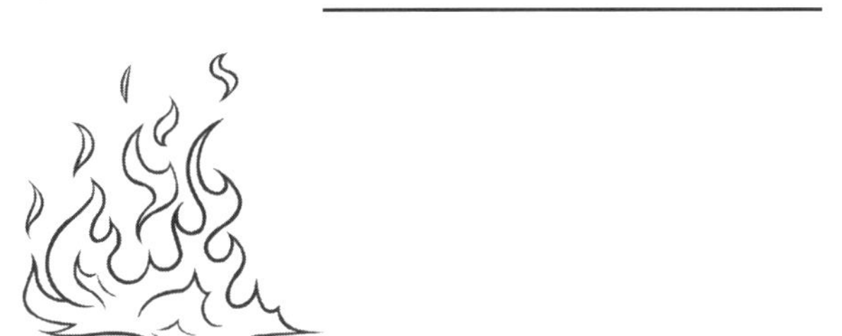

____

____

____

____

Lesson 79 the sound **ell**

Learning objectives

Children will:

- read and write words with the rime ell.
- identify the words when, who, what, where.

Australian Curriculum Content Descriptions

Sound and letter knowledge

ACELA1439 listen to the sounds a student hears in the word, and write letters to represent those sounds; identify rhyme and syllables in spoken words; identify and manipulate sounds (phonemes) in spoken words

Expressing and developing ideas

ACELA1434 explore spoken, written and multimodal texts and identify elements, for example words and images

ACELA1437 build vocabulary through multiple speaking and listening experiences

ACELA1438 build word families using onset and rime

ACELA1758 recognise the most common sound made by each letter of the alphabet, including consonants and short vowel sounds; know that spoken words are written down by listening to the sounds heard in the word and then writing letters to represent those sounds

Sight words

when, who, what, where

Word families

well, bell, tell, yell, shell, yellow, sell, smell

Vocabulary words

black, white, spotty, hen, sheep, horses, goats, pigs, cows

Extra assistance

At the end of *tell* is one sound made with two letters - ll. To reinforce the idea that two letters can make one sound, have students make crazy creatures by providing them with different animal heads with consonant sounds (b, h, p, s, t, w) written on them, bodies with vowels (a, e, i) on them and tails with *ll* or *ck*. Students make words using three sounds, creating crazy combination creatures and in the process reinforcing the idea that two letters can make one sound.

Classroom activities

Show me the Word!

Give each student a card with the word *what* on one side and the word *when* on the other. The teacher says an answer to a *what* or *when* question, for example: It is a button. A green dragon lives here. At nine o'clock. It will be on tomorrow.

Students hold up their card to show which type of question is being asked. Discuss their answers as a class.

Reading Eggs Lesson sequence	TEACH Content and skills	PRACTISE Children will:	APPLY
Hear: *Animated Lesson*	Introduce the word *when*.	identify and read the word *when* in isolation and in a sentence.	**Worksheet 1** Sight words
Write: *Word Family, Tiles*	Identify the correct onset letter to complete the word. Blend and recognise words.	choose the correct initial letter to make the word. Blend sounds to make the word.	**Worksheet 2** Word families
Find: *Time for 20, Rhyme Time*	Recognise a given word. Identify rhyming words.	find the given word in a group. Find images of rhyming words.	**Worksheet 3** Vocabulary
Vocabulary: *Find Your Treasure, Today's Words, Word Windows, City Zoo, Break it Up, Power Words*	Build vocabulary skills: Recognise key vocabulary. Blend and recognise words. Identify the number of phonemes in a word.	match pictures to words. Tap on the word being said. Blend sounds to read words. Identify the number of sounds in a word.	**Worksheet 4** Check
Read: *I Read You Read, Bubble Popper, Book*	Read sentences using basic vocabulary. Read aloud book.	listen, follow the reading and read along. Read and follow instructions.	**Reading Eggs book** Word families for ed, en, et, eg, ell

Classroom activities

Make it!

Give each student some playdough, plasticine or clay to make the rime *ell*. Then ask them to shape an onset letter to make a word. How many *ell* words can they make out of their materials?

They could also collect natural items such as leaves and twigs to combine with their modelling material to make *ell* words.

Related Reading Eggs Activities, Interactives, Songs and Books

Driving Tests

Test 4

Sight words: where, when, who, what

Letters and sounds: pig

Spelling Bank

Reading Eggs Puzzle Park

More than One

Animal Colour

Colour Code

Animal Fun

Reading Eggs Posters

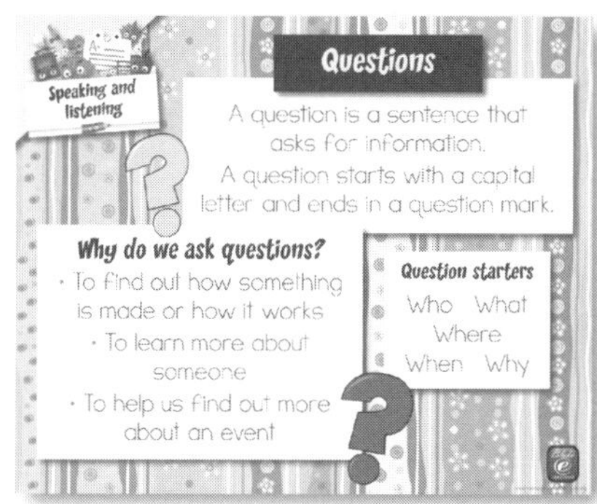

Reading Eggs Library Books

My Program Books

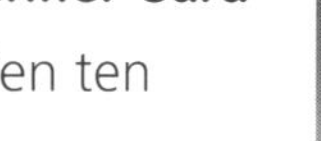

Critter Card

Zen ten

Teacher Toolkit

Spelling Activities

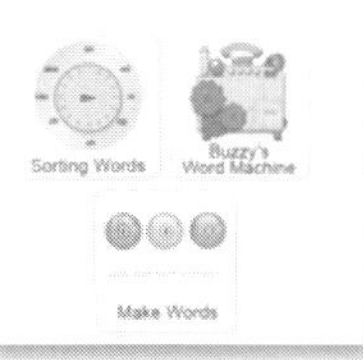

Reading Eggs Apps

Eggy Sight words

Eggy Snap

Sight words

Lesson 79 • Worksheet 1

Name

1 Trace and copy.

who

what

when

where

2 Read each sentence. Is it telling us **who**, **what**, **when** or **where**? Label it.

There is a party. ________________

The party is at 8. ________________

The king is coming. ________________

It is at the castle. ________________

Name

Word families

ell

Lesson 79 • Worksheet 2

1 Put the letters through the word machine. Write the words you make.

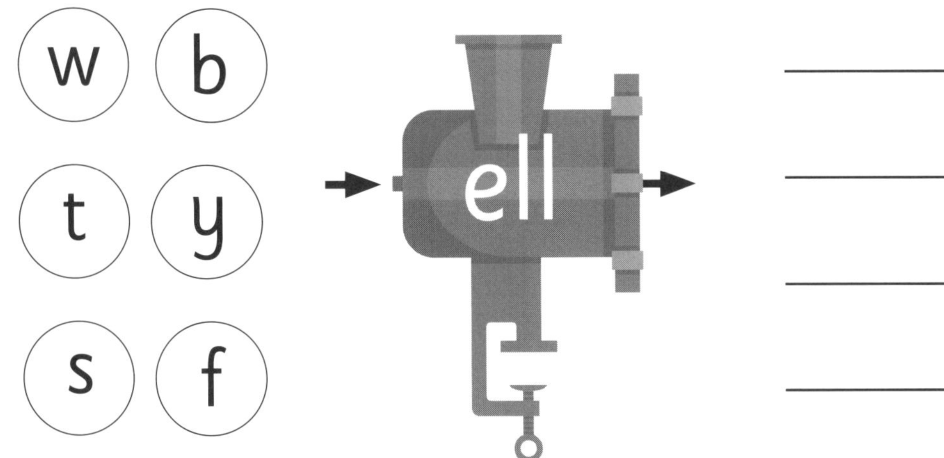

____

____

____

____

____

____

2 Finish the **ell** words.

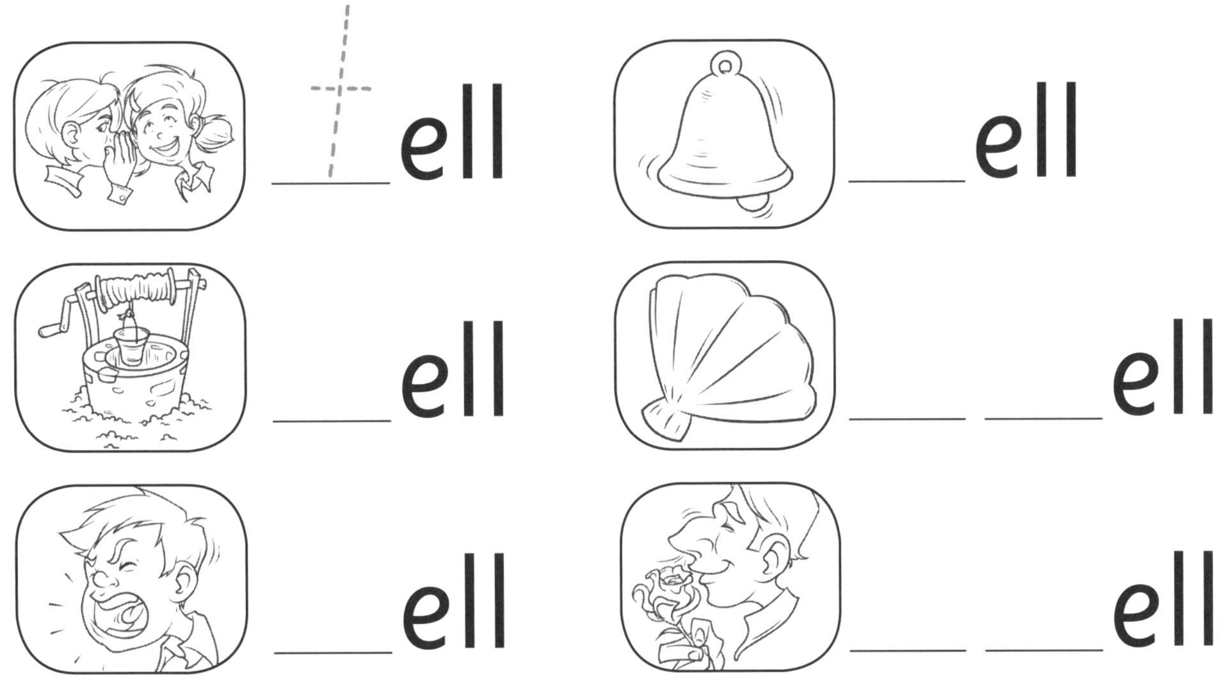

3 How many yellow things can you name?

____

Vocabulary

Name

Lesson 79 • Worksheet 3

1 Match each word to a picture.

2 Who lives here? Match the animals above to their homes.

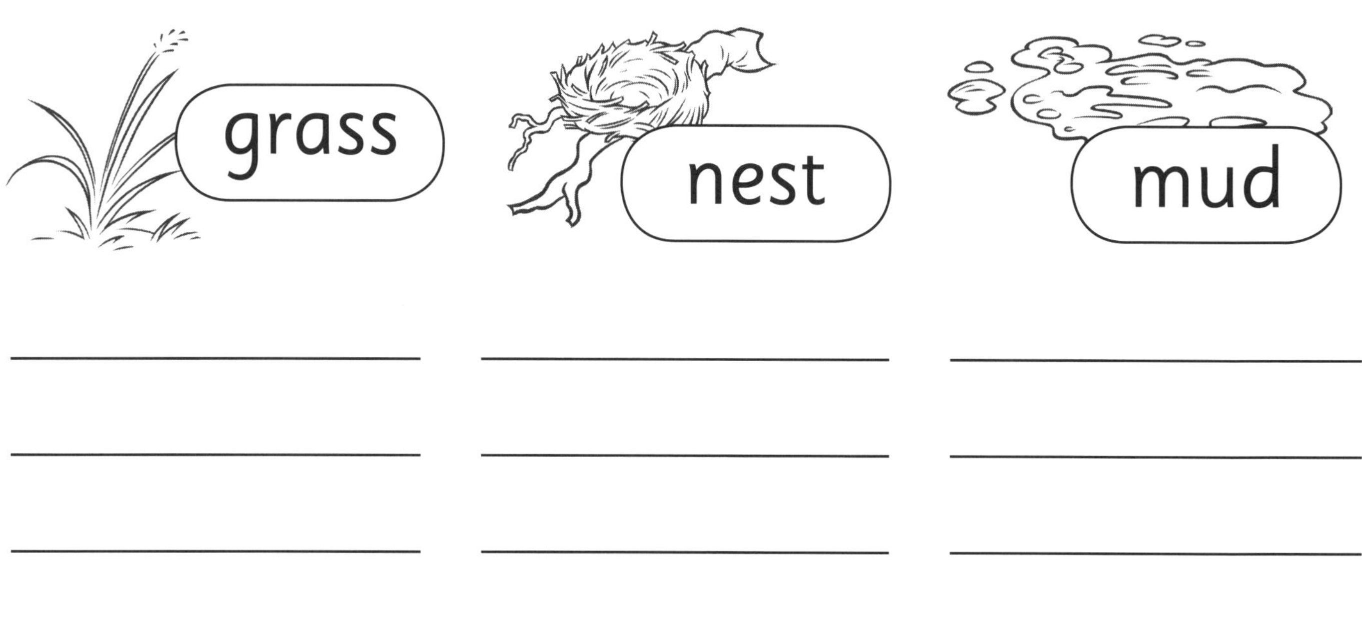

Name

Check

Lesson 79 • Worksheet 4

1 Trace.

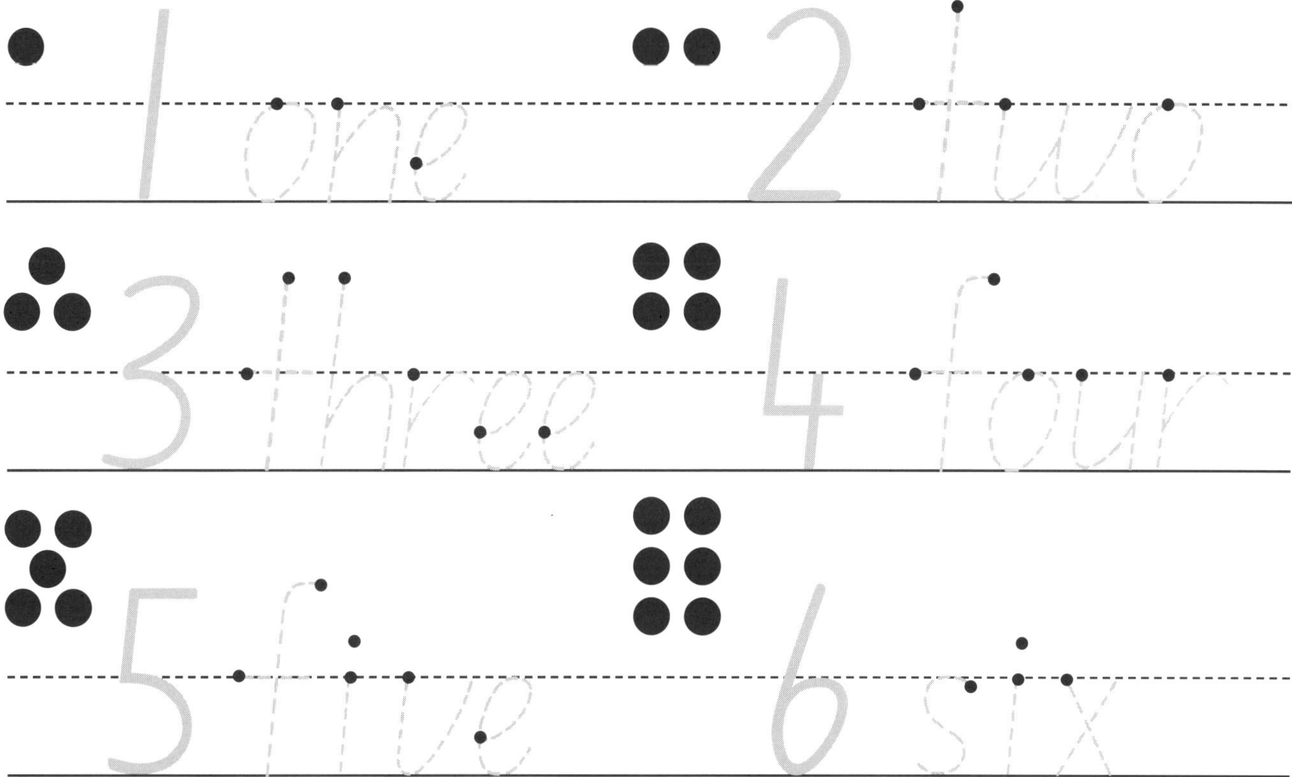

2 Follow the instructions to colour the pictures.

The cow is white and has black spots.

The pig is pink and has brown mud spots.

Lesson 80 Review

Learning objectives

Children will:

- revise all known word families.
- read and write words in a birthday party theme.

Australian Curriculum Content Descriptions

Sound and letter knowledge

ACELA1439 listen to the sounds a student hears in the word, and write letters to represent those sounds; identify rhyme and syllables in spoken words; identify and manipulate sounds (phonemes) in spoken words; identify onset and rime in one-syllable spoken words

Expressing and developing ideas

ACELA1437 build vocabulary through multiple speaking and listening experiences

ACELA1438 build word families using onset and rime

ACELA1758 recognise the most common sound made by each letter of the alphabet, including consonants and short vowel sounds; write consonant-vowel-consonant words by writing letters to represent the sounds in the spoken words; know that spoken words are written down by listening to the sounds heard in the word and then writing letters to represent those sounds

Word families

short a, e, i, o, u; word families

Vocabulary words

birthday, party, seven, plate

Extra assistance

To encourage students to distinguish vowel sounds aurally, play games where they must listen to and identify or spell a word correctly. A good game for this is Vowel Bingo. Have students fill in a nine-square grid with vowel sounds. They must listen to the teacher say a word (a CVC, CCVC or CVCC word) and distinguish which vowel sound is used. Then they cross out that vowel sound on their grid. First to have nine crosses calls out Bingo. The teacher should keep a hidden list of the vowels used so they can check the winner's card.

Classroom activities

CVC Triplets

Give two thirds of the class a consonant on a card. Give the other third of the class a vowel on a card. Ask students to form a trio and make a CVC word with their cards. (Have some spare cards to swap for students who are unable to make a word at the end.) The trio should write their word on a piece of paper, then illustrate it. Each trio presents their word to the class and explains what the word means.

Reading Eggs Lesson sequence	TEACH Content and skills	PRACTISE Children will:	APPLY
Hear: *Animated Lesson*	Revise making words using onset and rime, and the song *Rhyme Time*.	match the onset letter and the rime to make words.	**Worksheet 1** Word families
Write: *Sound Streamers, Tiles, Word Ladders*	Identify sounds in words.	sound out and select letters to make words.	**Worksheet 2** Read and write
Find: *Driving Trucks, What's Missing?*	Recognise a given word. Identify the missing sound in a word.	find the given word in a group. Choose the correct letter to make the word.	**Worksheet 3** Vocabulary
Vocabulary: *Make a Monster, Power Words, Find Your Treasure, Words per Minute*	Build vocabulary skills: Recognise key vocabulary.	read and follow instructions. Match pictures to words.	**Worksheet 4** Check
Read: *Book Ends, Book*	Read sentences using basic vocabulary. Read aloud book.	choose a word to finish the sentence. Listen, follow the reading and read along.	**Reading Eggs Story book** Meg's birthday

Classroom activities

Get it Wrong!

Put students in pairs with one sheet of paper and a pencil. Fold the paper down the middle to make two columns headed Wrong and Right. One student writes a sight word incorrectly in the Wrong column and the other has to correct it from memory in the Right column. If there is a dispute over correct spelling, they should bring it to the teacher. They then swap roles and continue writing words until the sheet is full.

Related Reading Eggs Activities, Interactives, Songs and Books

Driving Tests

Test 3

Sight words: not, his, that

Letters and sounds: bat, bug, tap, mat, egg, cat, car, sit, stop, fig, fan, nap, dog, doll, log, pet, pot, vet, ring, rat, get, yell, yet, at, hot, wet, jet, jug

Content words: seven

Spelling Bank

Reading Eggs Puzzle Park

More than One

What is it?

Squares

Teddy Bear

Music Café

Rhyme Time

Reading Eggs Posters

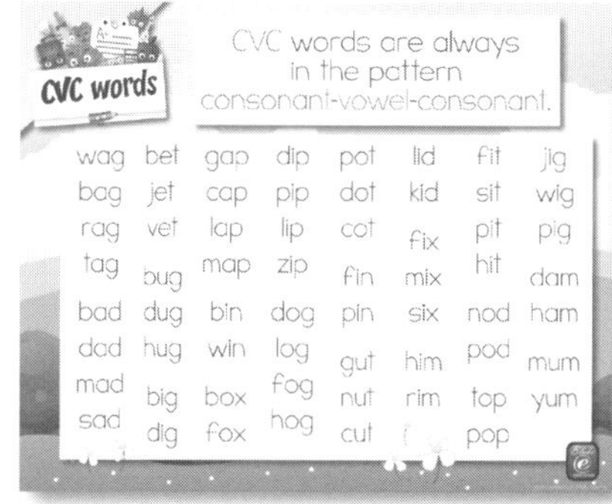

Reading Eggs Library Books

My Program Books

Critter Card

Alphapet

Teacher Toolkit

Spelling Activities

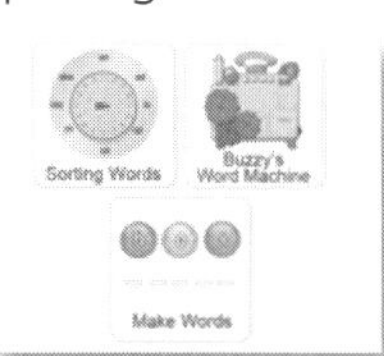

Reading Eggs Apps

Eggy Sight words

Eggy Snap

Review

Lesson 80 · Worksheet 1

Name

Word families

1 Sort these words into their word families.

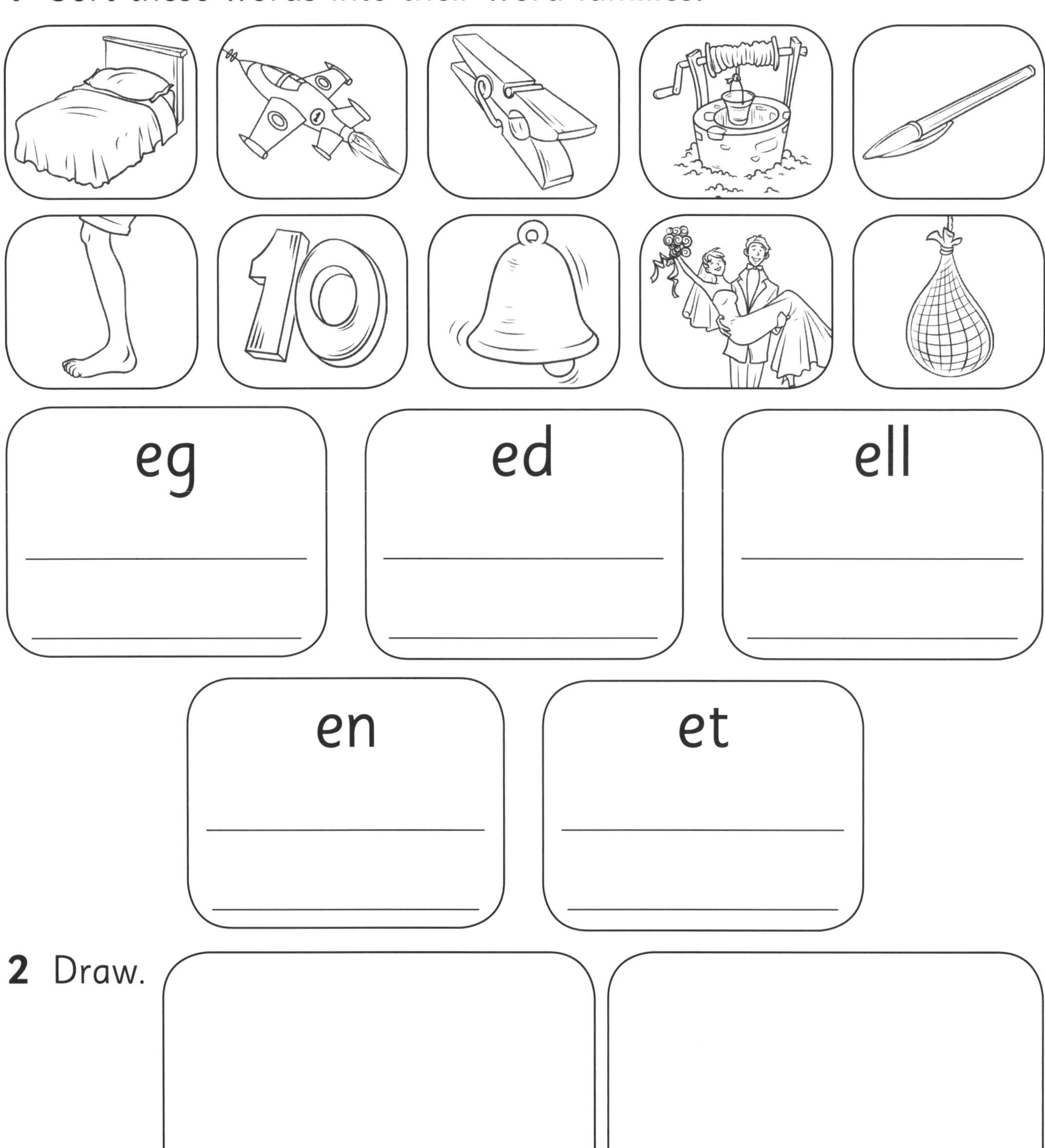

2 Draw.

six yellow pets

ten red eggs

Name

Read and write

Review

Lesson 80 • Worksheet 2

1 Complete the sentences. Use every word once.

party birthday cups plate and
seven Meg Sam bags hat hats

__________ is having a __________
__________ .

Meg has __________ plates, seven __________ , seven __________ and seven __________ .

__________ gets a __________ , a cup, a __________ __________ a bag.

2 Read and draw.

seven green hats	three green plates

Review

Name

Lesson 80 · Worksheet 3

Vocabulary

1 Match each picture to a word.

2 Match each word to a number.

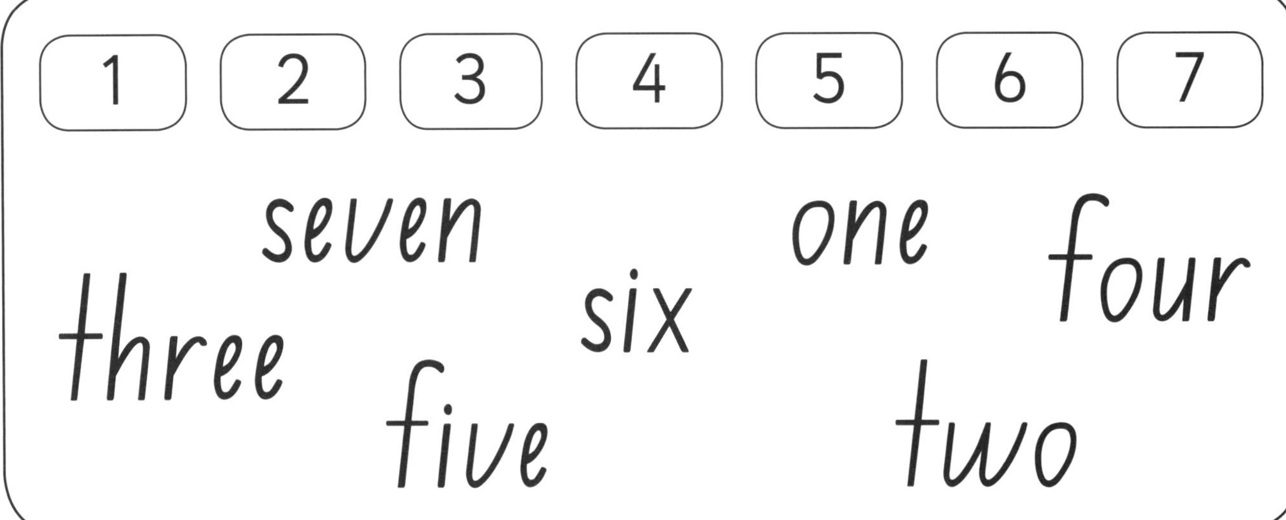

3 Colour the party words **red** and the number words **blue**.

one	party	five	hat	six
bag	birthday	ten	two	band

Name

Check

Review

Lesson 80 • Worksheet 4

Follow the instructions to set the table for the party. Colour the plates yellow. Draw seven red cups. Put seven pink candles on the cake. Colour the cake in blue and purple. Draw seven green hats.

Lesson 81 the word **with**

Learning objectives

Children will:

- revise consonant-vowel-consonant words.
- read and write using the word with.
- recognise and read words associated with the five senses.

Australian Curriculum Content Descriptions

Sound and letter knowledge

ACELA1439 listen to the sounds a student hears in the word, and write letters to represent those sounds; identify and manipulate sounds (phonemes) in spoken words; identify onset and rime in one-syllable spoken words

ACELA1457 replace sounds in spoken words (for example replace the *m* in mat with *c* to form a new word cat)

Expressing and developing ideas

ACELA1435 learn that word order in sentences is important for meaning

ACELA1437 build vocabulary through multiple speaking and listening experiences

ACELA1758 write consonant-vowel-consonant words by writing letters to represent the sounds in the spoken words; know that spoken words are written down by listening to the sounds heard in the word and then writing letters to represent those sounds

ACELA1778 learn an increasing number of high frequency sight words recognised in shared texts and in texts being read independently

Sight words

with

Word families

short vowel sounds

Vocabulary words

senses, see, taste, touch, smell, hearing, tongue, hand, nose, ear, eye, butterfly, flower, apple, sand

Extra assistance

The five senses are a great topic. Set up a station for each of the senses with items for students to taste, hear, look at, touch and smell. Ask the class to show you what category an item should go in by holding their nose, hand to the ear, making binoculars with their hands around their eyes, wriggling their fingers and sticking out their tongues. Play I Spy, pass around some Feely Bags with interesting items in them, make musical instruments, compile lists of Yuck and Yum tastes and Stinky and Good smells.

Classroom activities

Question and Answer

Write the question: What can you hear? on the board and brainstorm a list of possible answers. Write the answer sentence starter: I can hear … Ask students to write the question and their own answer. Extend this activity by asking them to write a question and answer for the other four senses on their own.

Reading Eggs Lesson sequence	TEACH Content and skills	PRACTISE Children will:	APPLY
Spell: *Rocket Launcher, Look, Listen and Spell*	Identify sounds in a word and make the word.	select the correct onset and rime. Select letters to spell a word.	**Worksheet 1** Word families
Find: *Shooting Stars*	Recognise a given word.	find the given word in a group.	**Worksheet 2** Sight words
Vocabulary: *Today's Topic Words, Power Words, Word Dominoes, Groups*	Build vocabulary skills: Recognise key vocabulary. Recognise categories of words.	match pictures to words. Match pictures to categories.	**Worksheet 3** Vocabulary
Write: *Bird Words*	Recognise correct word order for a sentence.	choose the correct words to make a sentence.	**Worksheet 4** Read and write
Read: *Book*	Read aloud book.	listen, follow the reading and read along.	**Reading Eggs nonfiction book** My five senses

Classroom activities

Flashcard Snap

Have at least two sets of flashcards for a short vowel word family. Shuffle and deal between two players. Keep cards face down. Players take turns to put a card from their pile onto a central pile, saying the word as they turn it over. If the two cards on top are the same, the players shout SNAP! The first to do so takes the central pile. Play continues until one player runs out of cards.

Related Reading Eggs Activities, Interactives, Songs and Books

Driving Tests

Test 5

Sight words: get, duck, dad, eyes, with car, will

Letters and sounds: log, bug, run, hot, kit, lip, tap, vet, box, yes, dog, egg, cat, fan, sat, jam, bag, win

Spelling Bank

Reading Eggs Puzzle Park

More than One

Finish the Alien

Sense it

Do You Know?

Reading Eggs Posters

Reading Eggs Library Books

My Program Books

Critter Card

Yabby dabby doo

Teacher Toolkit

- Spelling Activities
- Grammar Lessons
- Comprehension Lessons
- Targeting Comprehension Interactively
- Targeting Text Interactively

Reading Eggs Apps

Eggy Sight words

Eggy Snap

Eggy Phonics 1

Word families

Lesson 81 • Worksheet 1

Name

Match an initial letter with an end sound. Write the word and draw a picture in each box.

h p l d

en	ip	og	uck

Name

Sight words

with

Lesson 81 • Worksheet 2

1 Trace and copy.

with

2 Find the words. Colour **with** red, **what** blue and **have** green.

w	i	t	h	w	h	a	t	h	a	v	e
h	a	v	e	w	i	t	h	w	h	a	t
w	h	a	t	h	a	v	e	w	i	t	h

3 Use the words **with**, **what** and **have** to complete the sentences.

I ____________ blue eyes.

I can see ____________ my eyes.

____________ do you smell with?

You smell ____________ your nose.

Vocabulary

Name

Lesson 81 • Worksheet 3

1 Join each word to a picture.

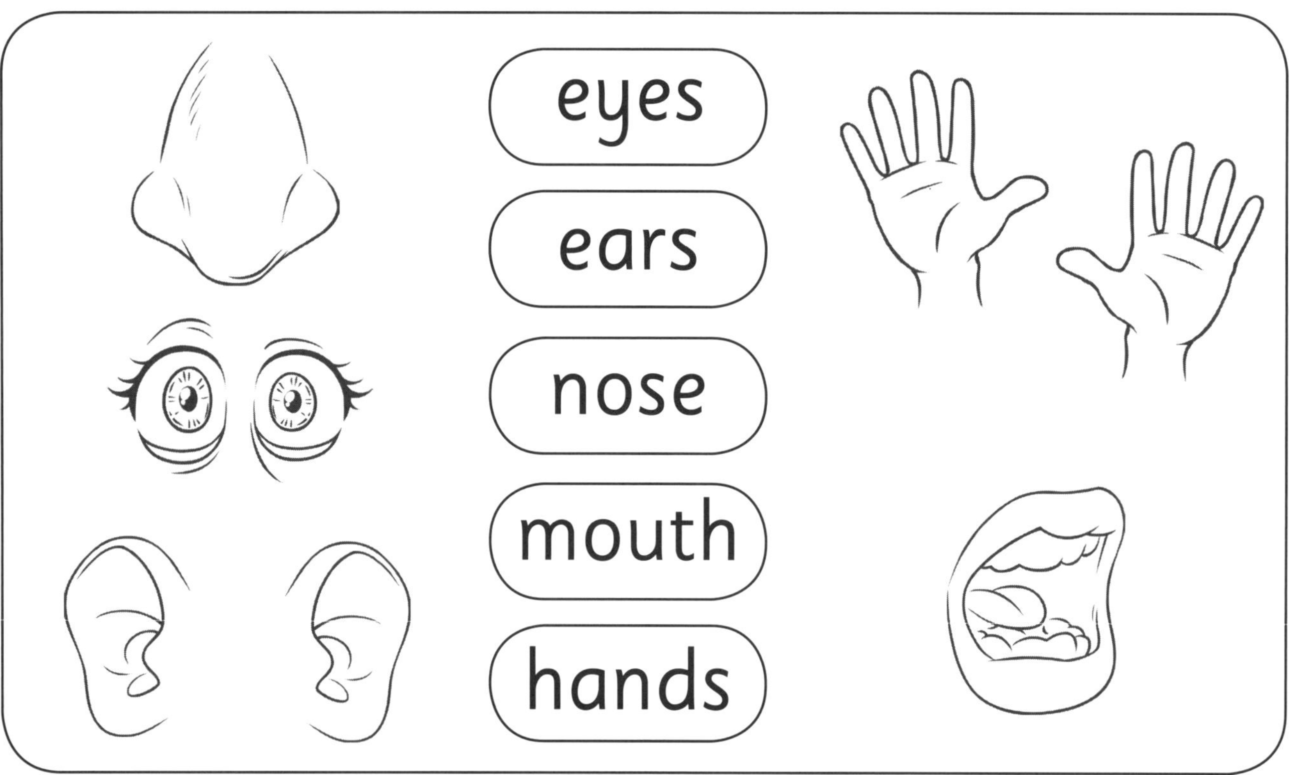

2 Label the picture.

hear see touch taste smell

h________

s________

s________

t________

t________

Name

Read and write

Lesson 81 • Worksheet 4

Complete the sentences.

eyes ears nose tongue hands

I can see with my

________________.

I can hear with my

________________.

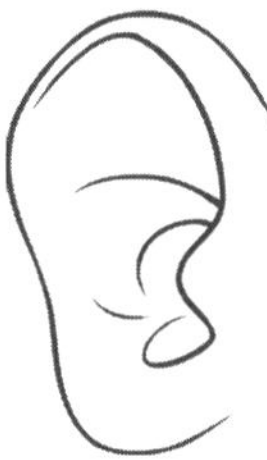

I can smell with my

________________.

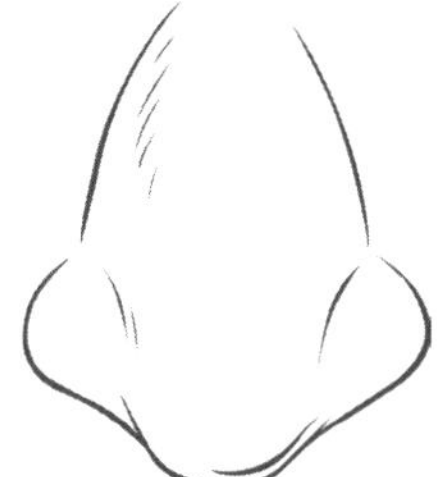

I can taste with my

________________.

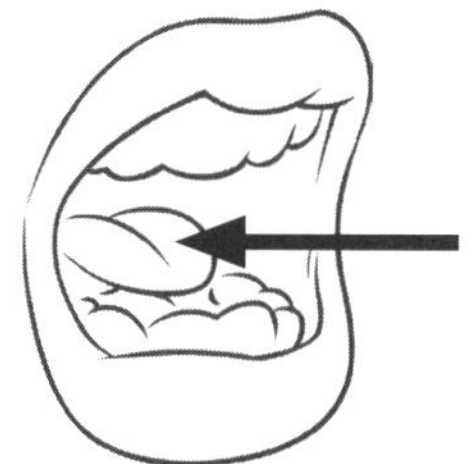

I can touch with my

________________.

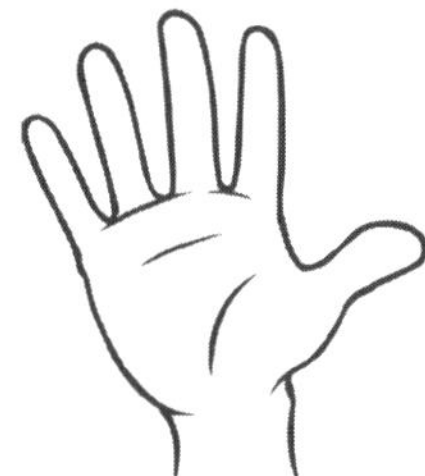

Lesson 82 the sound **ie**

Learning objectives

Children will:

- identify the sound ie as in pie and smile.
- recognise and read the word want.

Australian Curriculum Content Descriptions

Sound and letter knowledge

ACELA1458 say words with the same rime as a given word; recognise sound-letter matches including common vowel and consonant digraphs and consonant blends

ACELA1459 recognise that letters can have more than one sound for example *i* in pit or pie

Expressing and developing ideas

ACELA1435 learn that word order in sentences is important for meaning

ACELA1455 use morphemes to read words (for example by recognising the 'stem' in words such as go/ing)

ACELA1778 learn an increasing number of high frequency sight words recognised in shared texts and in texts being read independently

Interpreting, analysing and evaluating

ACELY1649 navigate a text correctly, starting at the right place and reading in the right direction, returning to the next line as needed, matching one spoken word to one written word

ACELY1659 combine knowledge of context, meaning, grammar and phonics to decode text

Text Structure and Organisation

ACELA1432 understand that punctuation is a feature of written text different from letters; recognise how capital letters are used for names, and that capital letters and full stops signal the beginning and end of sentences

Sight words

want, going, where

Word families

pie, lie, crocodile, smile

Vocabulary words

peach, plum, apple, shop, picnic

Extra assistance

In this lesson the idea of long vowel sounds is introduced. It is important to stress to students that the long i sound is made in this case by the digraph *ie*. This is two letters functioning as a single unit to make one sound. It is not an *i* and a silent *e*. Be sure to give them time to practise their pronunciation of the long i sound and compare it with the short i sound. Use pairs of words to contrast: pie and pit, lie and lip, die and dig

Classroom activities

Which Hat?

Place two hats on the floor with the labels short i and long i. Discuss the sounds. Have a pile of objects or pictures of objects that have the short i or the long i sound. Each student chooses one object or picture and works out which hat it must go in. Discuss their choice with the class.

Reading Eggs Lesson sequence	TEACH Content and skills	PRACTISE Children will:	APPLY
Hear: *Animated Lesson*	Introduce the sound *ie* through the words *pie* and *lie* and the song *I like apple pie*.	identify and read the words *pie* and *lie* in groups and in sentences.	**Worksheet 1** Word families
Write: *Pick Up Bricks, Write the Banner*	Recognise correct word order for a sentence.	choose the correct words to make a sentence.	**Worksheet 2** Read and write
Find: *Squirter*	Recognise a given word.	find the given word in a group.	**Worksheet 3** Vocabulary
Vocabulary: *Today's Topic Words, Today's Words, Make a Monster, Words per Minute*	Build vocabulary skills: Recognise key vocabulary.	match pictures to words. Tap on the word being said. Read and follow instructions.	**Worksheet 4** Check
Read: *Book*	Read aloud book.	listen, follow the reading and read along.	**Reading Eggs Story book** The pie shop

Classroom activities

Sentence Shuffle

Write and jumble an enlarged version of the sentence: But where is my apple pie? Read it with the children and ask them to work out the correct order. Reproduce each word on smaller pieces of card for each student. Suggest clues such as capital letters and question marks. Discuss the sentence when they are done.

Related Reading Eggs Activities, Interactives, Songs and Books

Spelling Bank

Map 6
Lesson 45
Focus sound words: line, mine, dice, mice, bite, kite, five

High frequency words: like, ride, white

Challenge: excite, fireworks

Driving Tests

Music Café

I like apple pie

Reading Eggs Puzzle Park

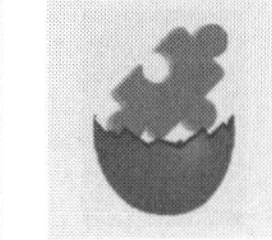

Colour Code

Animal Colours

What is it?

Reading Eggs Posters

Reading Eggs Library Books

My Program Books

Critter Card

Smile the crocodile

Teacher Toolkit

- Spelling Activities
- Grammar Lessons
- Comprehension Lessons
- Targeting Comprehension Interactively
- Targeting Text Interactively

Reading Eggs Apps

Eggy Sight words

Eggy Snap

Eggy Phonics 2

ie

Lesson 82 · Worksheet 1

Name

Word families

1 Colour the word **pie**.

2 Circle the **ie** words.

pin pie six lit lie
pit fig tie bit die

3 Write out the **ie** words.

__________ __________ __________ __________

4 Get Smile the crocodile to his pie. Follow the trail of **ie** words.

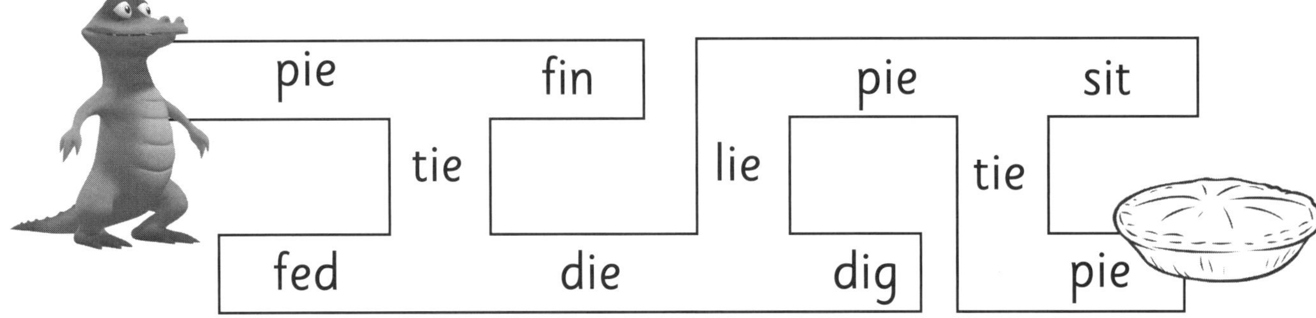

Name

Read and write

Lesson 82 • Worksheet 2

1 Put the words in order to make each sentence.

is a pie. little Here

pie. Here a red is

2 Draw a picture to go with this sentence.

Smile the crocodile is going to a picnic.

Vocabulary

Lesson 82 · Worksheet 3

Name

1 Match the words to their pictures.

picnic shop crocodile apple pie smile

2 Label the pies.

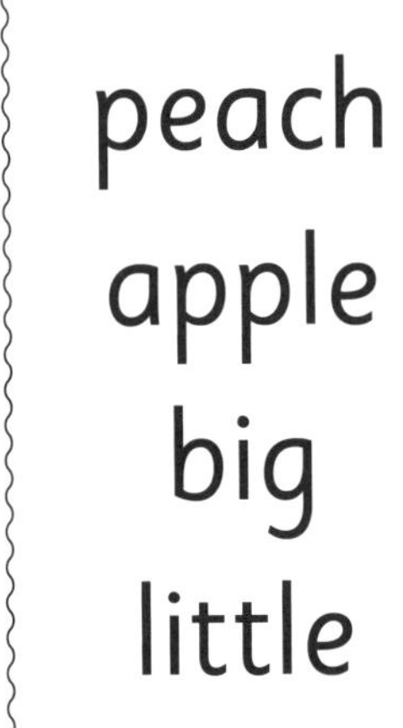

peach
apple
big
little

__________ pie __________ pie

__________ pie __________ pie

Name

Check

Lesson 82 · Worksheet 4

1 Finish each sentence and draw a picture.

big little red blue

I want a ______________ ,

______________ pie.

I want a ______________ ,

______________ pie.

2 Circle the rhyming words in each line.

fin smile picnic crocodile

lie lick tie tick pie

3 Decorate the pies.

Lesson 83 the sound **i-e**

Learning objectives

Children will:

- identify the split digraph i-e as in line.
- read and write the word help.

Australian Curriculum Content Descriptions

Sound and letter knowledge

ACELA1457 replace sounds in spoken words (for example replace the 'm' in mat with 'c' to form a new word cat)

ACELA1458 say words with the same rime as a given word; recognise sound-letter matches including common vowel and consonant digraphs and consonant blends

ACELA1459 recognise that letters can have more than one sound for example 'i' in pit, pie, pile

Expressing and developing ideas

ACELA1435 learn that word order in sentences is important for meaning

ACELA1758 know that spoken words are written down by listening to the sounds heard in the word and then writing letters to represent those sounds

ACELA1778 learn an increasing number of high frequency sight words recognised in shared texts and in texts being read independently

Interpreting, analysing and evaluating

ACELY1649 navigate a text correctly, starting at the right place and reading in the right direction, returning to the next line as needed, matching one spoken word to one written word

ACELY1659 combine knowledge of context, meaning, grammar and phonics to decode text

Word families

lie, line, mine, like, bike, hike, ride

Vocabulary words

family, parents, mother, father, sister, brother, homework, garden, table, help, walk, shoe

Extra assistance

For English language learners it is useful to provide rules they can follow in order to spell most words correctly. For ESL students rules also help with their pronunciation. In this case, the rule is making the long i sound with *ie* but with a consonant between them, as in *like* or *mine*. The sound is still the digraph *ie* but now it is *i-e* – a split digraph. It is not a silent e; the *ie* is one unit of sound that has been split up.

Classroom activities

Rhyme Time

Write the word *like* on the whiteboard and ask the class to say as many words as they can that rhyme with it. Write these on the board to make a word family. Write the words *hide* and *line* on the board. Ask the students to each choose a word family and write as many words as they can. Discuss responses with the class.

Bingo!

Give students a laminated board with ten squares on it. Ask them to write a word in each square which uses the *i-e* split digraph (use whiteboard markers). The teacher calls out words which use the *i-e* split digraph. Students put a cross on that word if they have it on their board. First one to ten calls out 'bingo' and wins!

Reading Eggs Lesson sequence	**TEACH Content and skills**	**PRACTISE Children will:**	**APPLY**
Hear: *Animated Lesson*	Introduce the sound *i-e* through the words *lie* and *line*.	select the letters which make the *ie* sound in *i-e* words.	**Worksheet 1** Word families
Write: *Pick Up Bricks*	Recognise correct word order for a sentence.	choose the correct words to make a sentence.	**Worksheet 2** Read and write
Find: *Driving Trucks, Hairy Heads*	Recognise a given word.	find the given word in a group.	**Worksheet 3** Vocabulary
Vocabulary: *Today's Topic Words, Power Words, Fishing Boats*	Build vocabulary skills: Recognise key vocabulary.	match pictures to words.	**Worksheet 4** Check
Read: *Book Ends, Book*	Read sentences using basic vocabulary. Read aloud book.	choose a word to finish the sentence. Listen, follow the reading and read along.	**Reading Eggs nonfiction book** Families help each other

Related Reading Eggs Activities, Interactives, Songs and Books

Driving Tests

Test 8

Content words; sister, brother, mother, father, family

Spelling Bank

Reading Eggs Puzzle Park

Transport

Dressing Up

What is it?

Reading Eggs Posters

Reading Eggs Library Books

My Program Books

Teacher Toolkit

- Spelling Activities
- Grammar Lessons
- Comprehension Lessons
- Targeting Comprehension Interactively
- Targeting Text Interactively

Reading Eggs Apps

Eggy Sight words

Eggy Snap

Eggy Phonics 2

Critter Card

Bow tie magpie

i-e

Lesson 83 • Worksheet 1

Name

Word families

1 Trace and copy.

lie line

2 Circle the letters that make the **long i** sound.

tie mine hike

3 Complete the **long i** words.

p______

b___k___

n___n___

4 Draw nine fine pies.

Name

Read and write

Lesson 83 • Worksheet 2

1 Match the sentences to their pictures.

I help my brother tie his shoe laces.

My father helps me ride my bike.

Our mother helps us with our homework.

2 Write a sentence using the words **help** and **sister**. Draw a picture.

Vocabulary

Lesson 83 · Worksheet 3

Name

1 Join each word to a picture.

2 Complete each sentence.

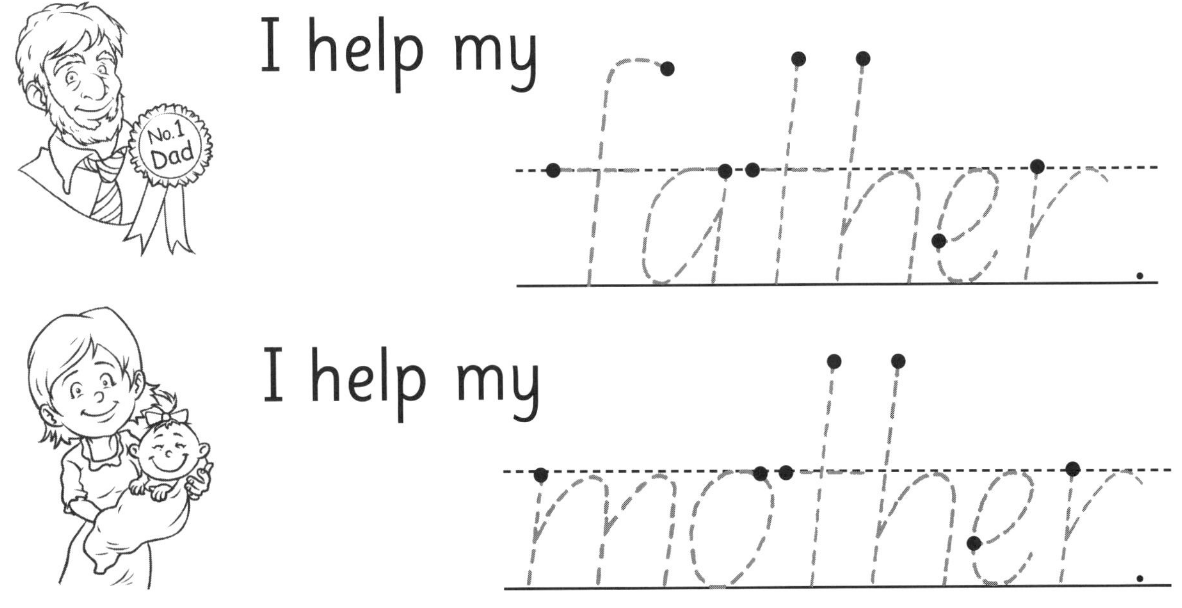

Name

Check

Lesson 83 · Worksheet 4

1 Match the jigsaw pieces and write the words.

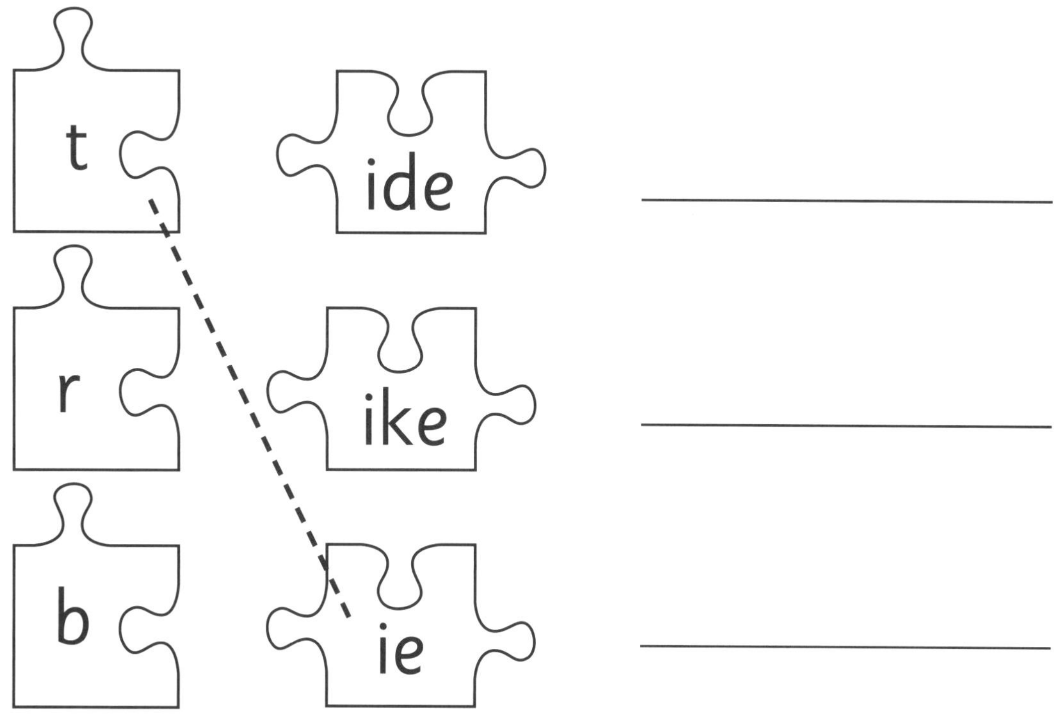

2 Guess the word by its shape. Write each word in the correct box.

help garden table walk

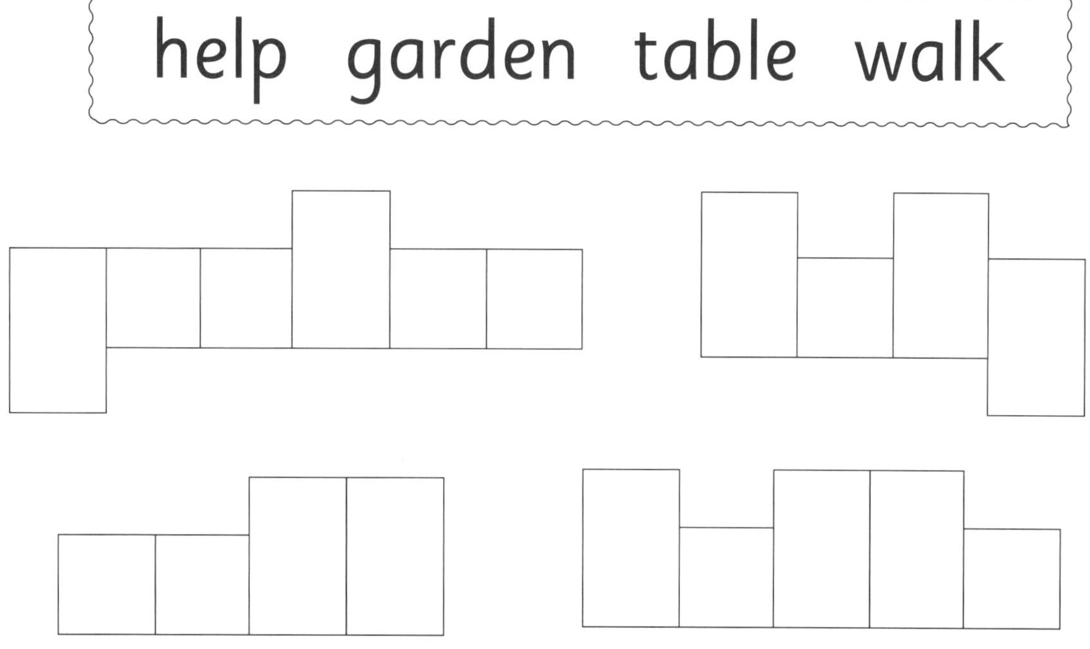

Lesson 84 the sound **ine**

Learning objectives

Children will:

- identify the rime ine.
- sort words that contain ie or i-e.
- read and write words about bike riding.

Australian Curriculum Content Descriptions

Sound and letter knowledge

ACELA1439 identify onset and rime in one-syllable spoken words

ACELA1458 say words with the same rime as a given word; recognise sound-letter matches including common vowel and consonant digraphs and consonant blends

Expressing and developing ideas

ACELA1435 learn that word order in sentences is important for meaning

ACELA1438 build word families using onset and rime

ACELA1455 using morphemes to read words (for example by recognising the 'stem' in words such as walk/ed)

ACELA1758 know that spoken words are written down by listening to the sounds heard in the word and then writing letters to represent those sounds

ACELA1778 learn an increasing number of high frequency sight words recognised in shared texts and in texts being read independently

Interpreting, analysing and evaluating

ACELY1649 navigate a text correctly, starting at the right place and reading in the right direction, returning to the next line as needed, matching one spoken word to one written word

ACELY1659 combine knowledge of context, meaning, grammar and phonics to decode text

Sight words

too, off, over

Word families

mine, nine, pine, fine, dine, line, spine, shine, vine, bike, strike, spike, hike, like, alike, pie, die, tie, lie

Vocabulary words

ride, crash, fall, track, Charlie, wobble

Extra assistance

Learning word families can provide students with an opportunity to start writing some rhymes of their own. Encourage them to write short sentences that end with rhyming words. Emphasise that the sentences should be related, for example:

This bike is mine.

It is fine.

This activity will encourage them to relate word families and rhyming words.

Classroom activities

Which Hat?

Place three hats on the floor with the labels *ine*, *ie* and *ide*. Discuss the sounds. Have a pile of objects or pictures of objects that end with *ine*, *ie* and *ide*. Each student chooses one and works out which hat it must go in. Discuss their choice with the class.

Reading Eggs Lesson sequence	TEACH Content and skills	PRACTISE Children will:	APPLY
Hear: *Animated Lesson*	Review the sound *i-e* through *ine* words.	select the letters which make the *ie* sound in *ine* words.	**Worksheet 1** Word families
Write: *Pick Up Bricks, Write the Banner*	Recognise correct word order for a sentence.	choose the correct words to make a sentence.	**Worksheet 2** Read and write
Find: *Word family, Bowling, Frog Logs, Shooting Stars*	Identify the correct onset letter to complete the word. Identify the rime in the word. Recognise a given word.	choose the correct initial letter to make the word. Match a word to its rime. Find the given word in a group.	**Worksheet 3** Vocabulary
Vocabulary: *Today's Topic Words*	Build vocabulary skills: Recognise key vocabulary.	match pictures to words.	**Worksheet 4** Check
Read: *Book*	Read aloud book.	listen, follow the reading and read along.	**Reading Eggs Story book** Charlie rides a bike

Classroom activities

Find the Start

Give students a list of words with the first letter missing. Ask them to figure out which letter could be the starter for all the given words, for example: _ie _ine _ile _ipe

Discuss the answers as a class. Was there more than one possible answer?

Related Reading Eggs Activities, Interactives, Songs and Books

Spelling Bank

Fish

Lesson 45

Focus sound words: line, mine, dice, mice, bite, kite, five

High requency words: like, ride, white

Challenge: excite, fireworks

Reading Eggs Puzzle Park

Transport

Do it

Do You Know?

Driving Tests

Reading Eggs Library Books

My Program Books

Reading Eggs Posters

Critter Card

Spiny porcupine

Teacher Toolkit

- Spelling Activities
- Grammar Lessons
- Comprehension Lessons
- Targeting Comprehension Interactively
- Targeting Text Interactively

Reading Eggs Apps

Eggy Sight words

Eggy Snap

Eggy Phonics 2

Word families

Lesson 84 • Worksheet 1

Name

1 Use the word wheels to make words.

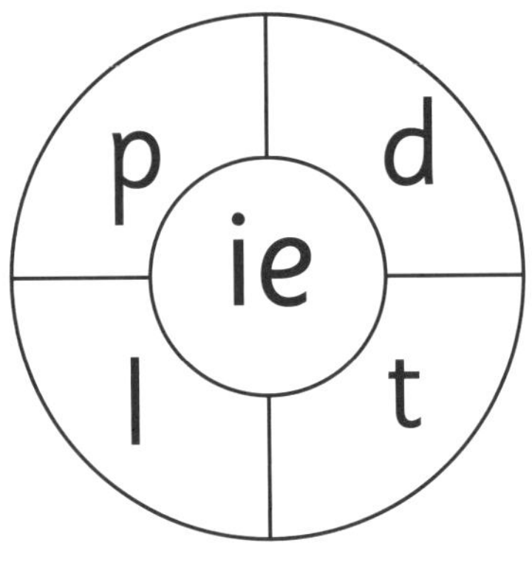

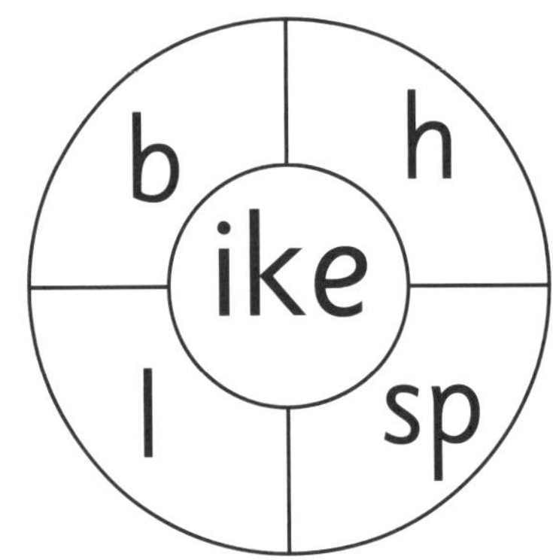

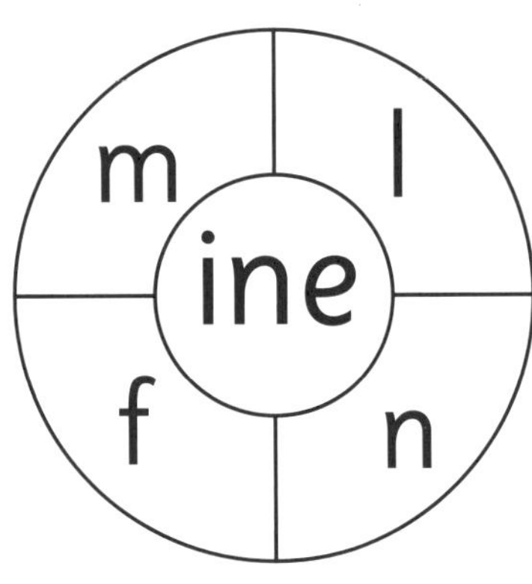

2 Colour the vowel sound.

ee a ie

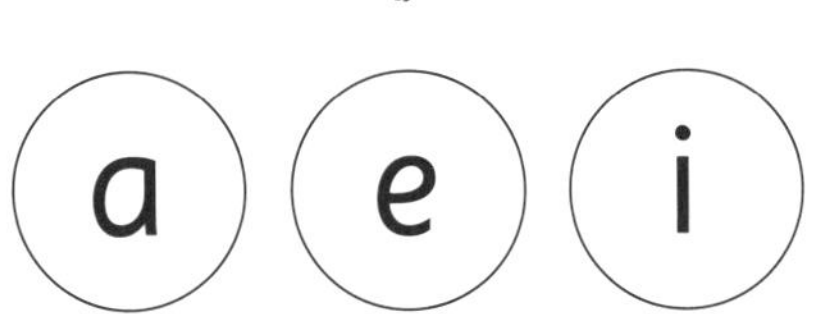

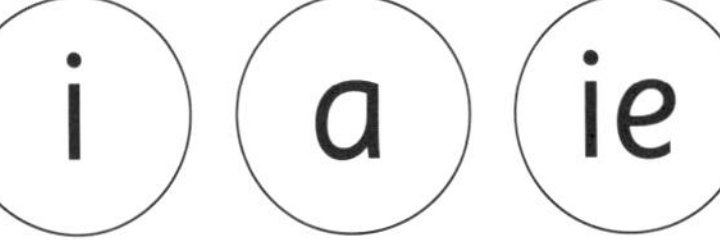

a e i

Name

Read and write

Lesson 84 • Worksheet 2

1 Circle the sentences that match the story.

Charlie likes his green car.
Charlie likes his red bike.

Charlie can ride his bike.
Charlie can ride his horse.

2 Complete the sentences.

off over too fall

This bike is __________ big.
Charlie fell __________ his bike.
The bike fell __________ .
He did not __________ off.

Vocabulary

Name

Lesson 84 • Worksheet 3

Colour the correct word. Cross out the wrong word.

Charlie wants to ride / crash his bike.

The bike wobbled / fell a bit.

Charlie fall / fell off the bike.

The bike went crash / truck .

Charlie does not want to fall / fell off.

Name

Check

Lesson 84 • Worksheet 4

1 Crack the code!

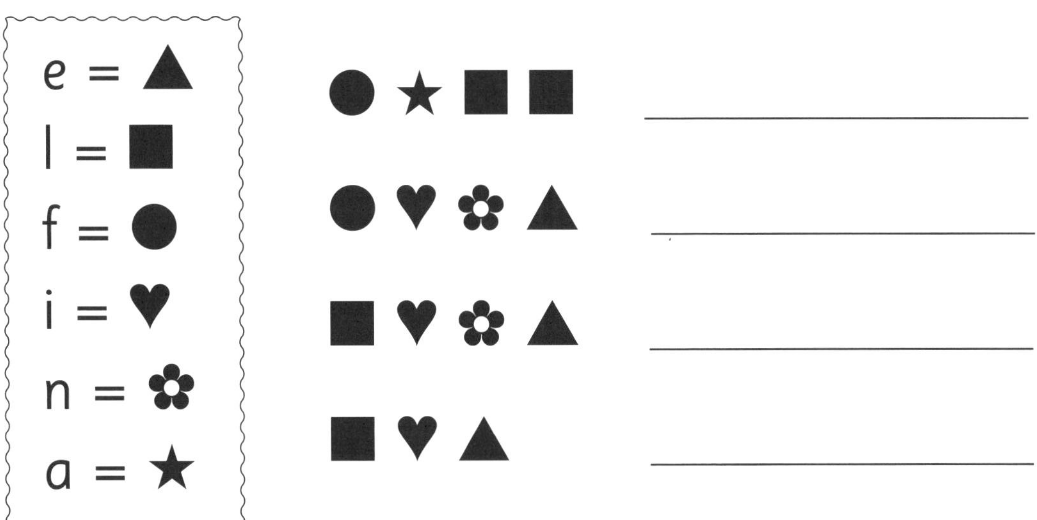

2 How many sounds can you hear in each word?
Colour the bubble.

fell	mine	track
2 3 4	2 3 4	3 4 5
off	**too**	**tie**
1 2 3	2 3 4	1 2 3

3 Get Spiny porcupine to his bike. Follow the trail of **ine** words.

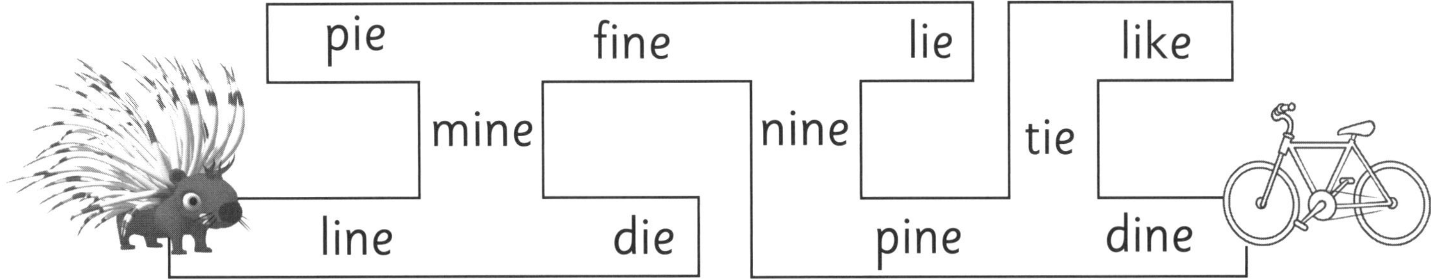

Lesson 85 the sound **sh**

Learning objectives

Children will:

- identify the sound sh.
- read and write sh words.

Australian Curriculum Content Descriptions

Sound and letter knowledge

ACELA1439 listen to the sounds a student hears in the word, and write letters to represent those sounds; identify and manipulate sounds (phonemes) in spoken words

ACELA1458 say words with the same rime as a given word; recognise sound-letter matches including common vowel and consonant digraphs and consonant blends

ACELA1459 recognise that letters can have more than one sound for example 'u' in cut, put, use

Expressing and developing ideas

ACELA1435 learn that word order in sentences is important for meaning

ACELA1438 build word families using onset and rime

ACELA1758 know that spoken words are written down by listening to the sounds heard in the word and then writing letters to represent those sounds

Interpreting, analysing and evaluating

ACELY1649 navigate a text correctly, starting at the right place and reading in the right direction, returning to the next line as needed, matching one spoken word to one written word

ACELY1659 combine knowledge of context, meaning, grammar and phonics to decode text

Text Structure and Organisation

ACELA1432 understand that punctuation is a feature of written text different from letters; recognise how capital letters are used for names, and that capital letters and full stops signal the beginning and end of sentences

Word families

shock, shirt, sheep, shark, shoes, shell, shop, shed, ship

Extra assistance

Many ESL students will use *sh* and *ch* interchangeably. To pronounce *sh* correctly, air is pushed out softly across the tongue and between slightly open teeth and pursed lips. The sound does not use the vocal chords (it is unvoiced) and should be a continuous flow of air. Let students practise pronunciation with pairs of words: ship and chip, shop and chop, share and chair.

Classroom activities

Search for a Sound

Give each student a page from a magazine, newspaper or photocopied page from a book and ask them to highlight as many words with *sh* as they can in three minutes. Ask each student to tell you a different word they found. Write a list on the board and discuss the words as you write them up.

Mind the Gap!

Write this sentence on the board: A shark in a ____. Read the sentence together and brainstorm a list of possible answers. Students then copy the sentence: A sheep on a ____. into their book and finish it with their choice of word and matching illustration.

Reading Eggs Lesson sequence	TEACH Content and skills	PRACTISE Children will:	APPLY
Hear: *Animated Lesson*	Introduce the sound *sh*.	identify the sound *sh* in a group and in words.	**Worksheet 1** Word families
Write: *Look, Listen and Spell, Bird Words*	Identify sounds in a word and write the word. Recognise correct word order for a sentence.	sound out a word and select letters to spell it correctly. Choose the correct words to make a sentence.	**Worksheet 2** Read and write
Find: *What's Missing?*	Identify the missing sound in a word.	choose the correct letter to make the word.	**Worksheet 3** Vocabulary
Vocabulary: *Today's Topic Words, Find Your Treasure, Power Words*	Build vocabulary skills: Recognise key vocabulary.	match pictures to words.	**Worksheet 4** Check
Read: *I Read You Read, Book*	Read sentences using basic vocabulary. Read aloud book.	listen, follow the reading and read along.	**Reading Eggs Story book** A shark in a shirt

Related Reading Eggs Activities, Interactives, Songs and Books

Spelling Bank

Elephants
Lesson 34
Focus sound words: ship, shop, shut

Driving Tests

Reading Eggs Puzzle Park

Animal Fun
Dressing Up
What is it?
More than One

Reading Eggs Posters

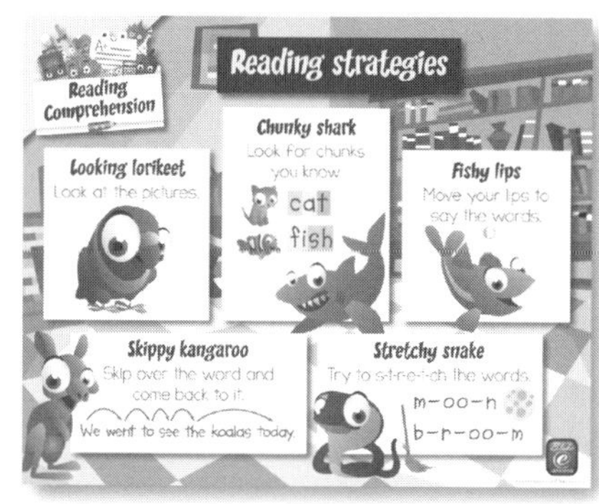

Reading Eggs Library Books

My Program Books

Teacher Toolkit

- Spelling Activities
- Grammar Lessons
- Comprehension Lessons
- Targeting Comprehension Interactively
- Targeting Text Interactively

Reading Eggs Apps

Eggy Sight words

Eggy Snap

Eggy Phonics 3

Eggy Vocab

Critter Card

Shelley shark

sh

Lesson 85 · Worksheet 1

Name

Word families

1 Join each word to a picture.

2 Complete each sentence and draw a picture.

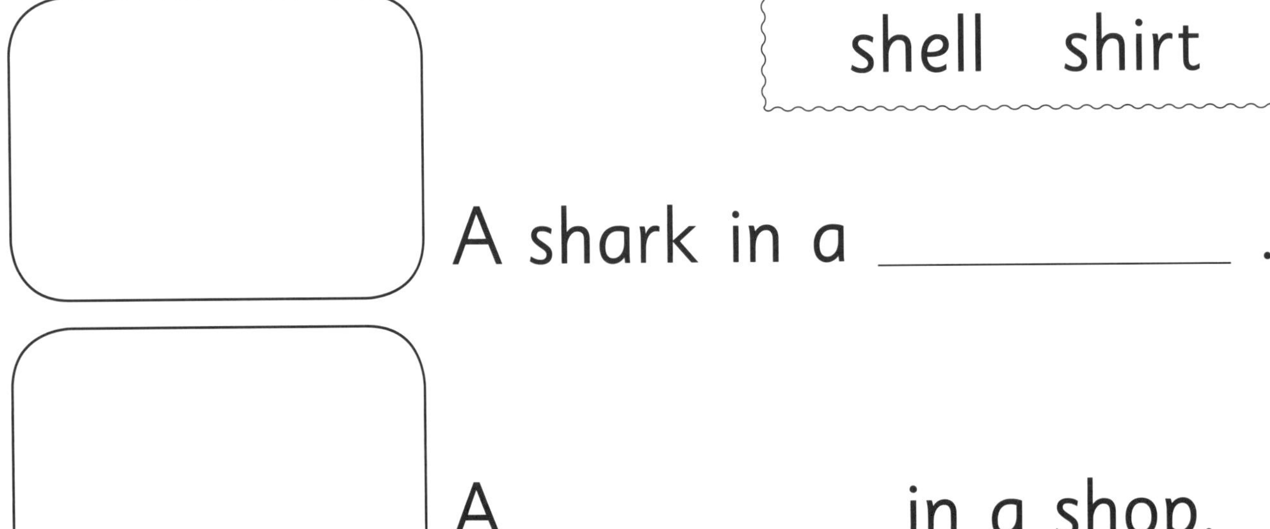

Name

Read and write

sh

Lesson 85 • Worksheet 2

1 Read and draw.

a shark on a shed	a sheep in shoes

2 Put the words in order to make each sentence.

a shop. shell in A

in shirt. shoes shark and A a

sh

Lesson 85 • Worksheet 3

Name

Vocabulary

1 Complete the words to label the pictures.

sh________

________ll

shar____

________ip

sh___p

shoe____

2 Write a sentence for each word.

shed

____

____

shirt

____

____

Name

Check

sh

Lesson 85 • Worksheet 4

1 Join the puzzle pieces. Write the words.

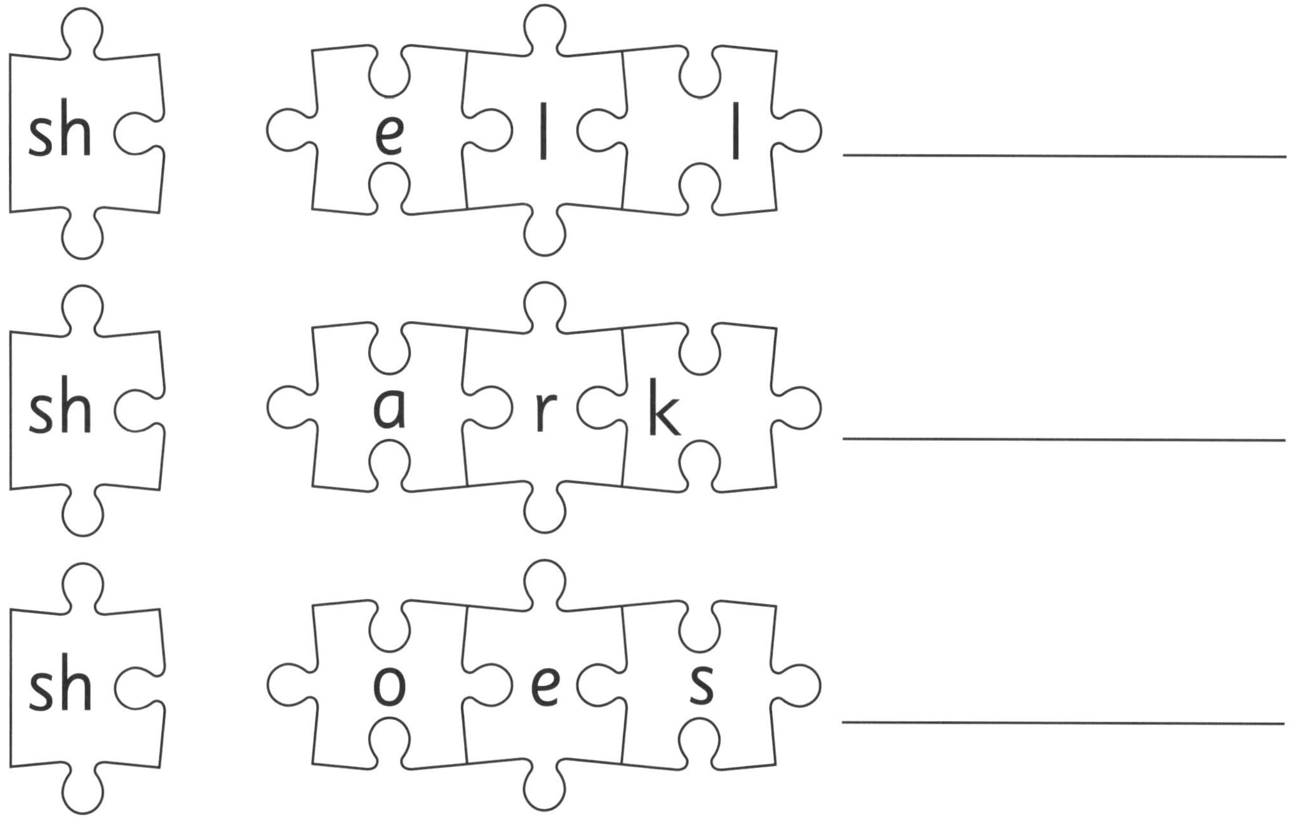

2 Colour the beginning sound.

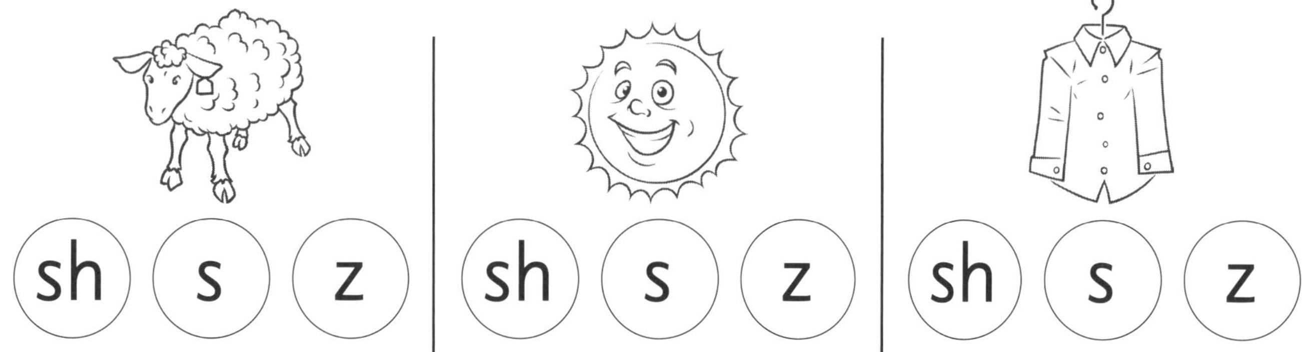

3 Guess the word by its shape. Write each word in the correct box.

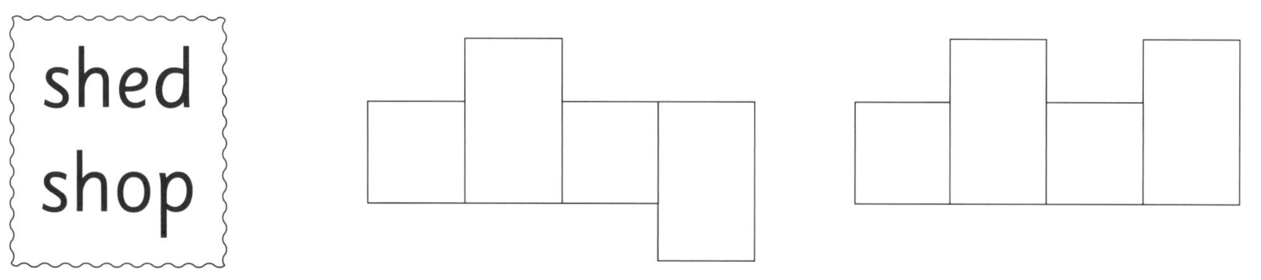

Lesson 86 the sound **sh**

Learning objectives

Children will:

- review the sound sh.
- read and write sh words.

Australian Curriculum Content Descriptions

Sound and letter knowledge

ACELA1439 identify and manipulate sounds (phonemes) in spoken words

ACELA1458 say words with the same rime as a given word; recognise sound-letter matches including common vowel and consonant digraphs and consonant blends

Expressing and developing ideas

ACELA1435 learn that word order in sentences is important for meaning

ACELA1438 build word families using onset and rime

ACELA1455 using morphemes to read words (for example by recognising the 'stem' in words such as walk/ed)

ACELA1758 know that spoken words are written down by listening to the sounds heard in the word and then writing letters to represent those sounds

ACELA1778 learn an increasing number of high frequency sight words recognised in shared texts and in texts being read independently

Interpreting, analysing and evaluating

ACELY1649 navigate a text correctly, starting at the right place and reading in the right direction, returning to the next line as needed, matching one spoken word to one written word

ACELY1659 combine knowledge of context, meaning, grammar and phonics to decode text

Text Structure and Organisation

ACELA1432 understand that punctuation is a feature of written text different from letters; recognise how capital letters are used for names, and that capital letters and full stops signal the beginning and end of sentences

Sight words

these

Word families

shop, shoe, shelf, shovel, shiny, sheep, ship, shirt, shell, sheet, shine, shorts, short, kite, pie, bike, nine, tie

Vocabulary words

laces, tried, buy, new

Extra assistance

Give students opportunities to practise pronunciation with repetition and choral response activities. Choral responses, where groups of students recite the same word, phrase, sentence or sound, are an effective tool to build familiarity with new sounds and vocabulary. Have the students repeat words after you to practise pronunciation.

Classroom activities

For Starters

Put the sound *sh* on the board in magnetic letters. Put all the letters of the alphabet around it. Students take turns to make *sh* words with the magnetic letters. Discuss their words and write a list.

Reading Eggs Lesson sequence	TEACH Content and skills	PRACTISE Children will:	APPLY
Hear: *Animated Lesson*	Review the sound *sh*.	identify the letters that make the sound *sh*. Make *sh* words.	**Worksheet 1** Word families
Write: *Write the Banner*	Recognise correct word order for a sentence.	choose the correct words to make a sentence.	**Worksheet 2** Read and write
Find: *Driving Trucks, Shooting Stars, Jumping Astronauts*	Recognise a given word.	find the given word in a group.	**Worksheet 3** Vocabulary
Vocabulary: *Today's Topic Words, Word Dominoes, Words per Minute*	Build vocabulary skills: Recognise key vocabulary.	match pictures to words.	**Worksheet 4** Check
Read: *Book*	Read aloud book.	listen, follow the reading and read along.	**Reading Eggs Story book** Shopping

Lesson 86

Classroom activities

Buzzy Bee

Sit in a circle. Everyone says, 'Buzzy Bee, Buzzy Bee, what have you got in your hive for me? Something beginning with *sh*!' Then students take turns around the circle naming something that begins with the sound /sh/.

Related Reading Eggs Activities, Interactives, Songs and Books

Driving Tests

Test 9

Letters and sounds: shop, wish, flash, push, shell, sh

Spelling Bank

Reading Eggs Puzzle Park

Dressing Up

Do You Know?

What is it?

More than One

Reading Eggs Posters

Reading Eggs Library Books

My Program Books

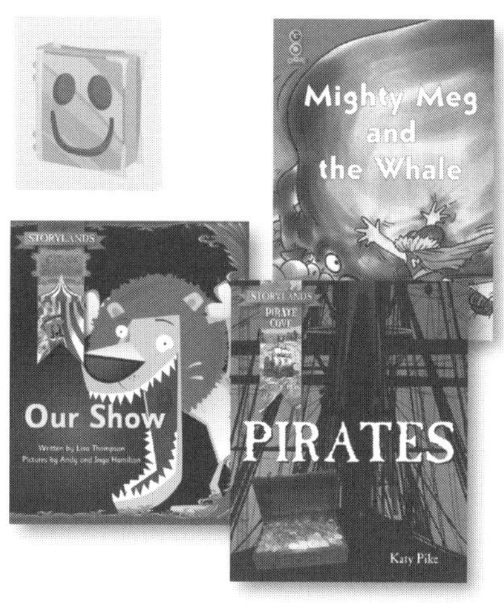

Teacher Toolkit

- Spelling Activities
- Grammar Lessons
- Comprehension Lessons
- Targeting Comprehension Interactively
- Targeting Text Interactively

Reading Eggs Apps

Eggy Sight words

Eggy Snap

Eggy Phonics 3

Eggy Vocab

Critter Card

Shoe sheep

Lesson 86 · Worksheet 1

Name

Word families

1 Join each word to a picture.

2 Colour the animal words **red** and the clothing words **blue**.

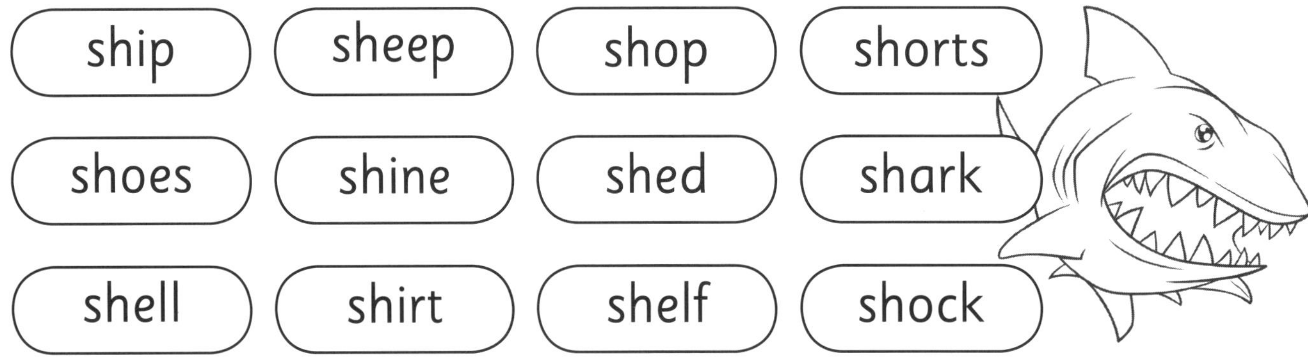

3 How many shiny things can you name?

Name

Read and write

sh

Lesson 86 · Worksheet 2

Complete the sentences.

shirt shiny shops shoes

Shelley shark is going to the

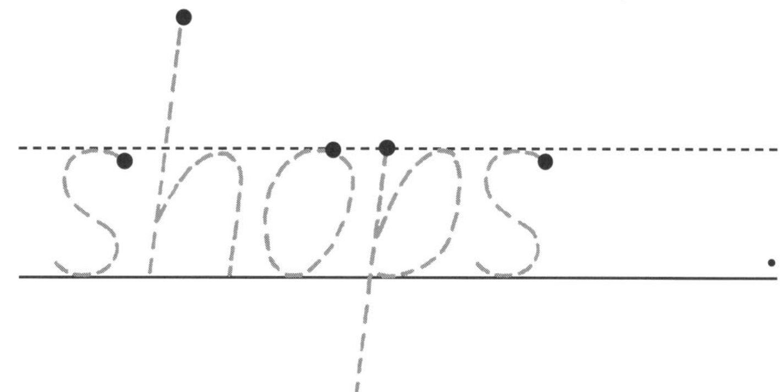

Shelley wants to buy a new

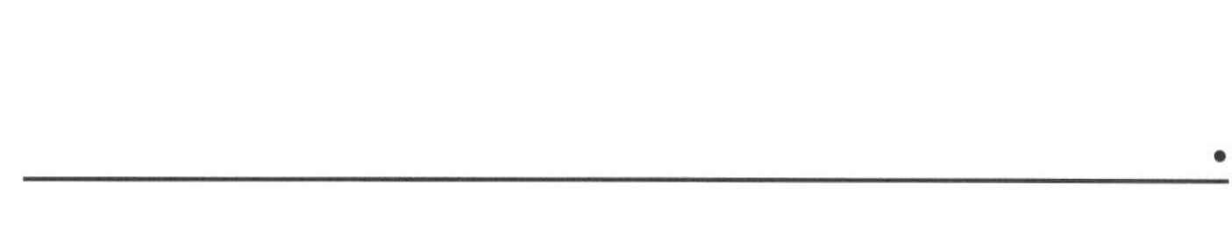

Shoe sheep wants to buy new

These shoes are very

sh

Lesson 86 • Worksheet 3

Name

Vocabulary

Put the words in order to make each sentence.

This short. shirt too is

shop. Let's into this go

shiny I these shoes. like

Name

Check

sh

Lesson 86 · Worksheet 4

1 Colour the correct word. Cross out the wrong word.

These / This shoes have shoelaces.

Shelley wants to buy / new a buy / new shirt.

These / This shirt has too many ships.

These shoes are very shine / shiny.

2 Circle the rhyming words in each line.

shine tin nine pine ship

shirt spike like spine bike

Lesson 87 the sound **i-e**

Learning objectives

Children will:

- identify the rimes that can be made with i-e.
- read and write i-e words.

Australian Curriculum Content Descriptions

Sound and letter knowledge

ACELA1439 listen to the sounds a student hears in the word, and write letters to represent those sounds; identify rhyme and syllables in spoken words; identify and manipulate sounds (phonemes) in spoken words

ACELA1457 recognise and produce rhyming words; replace sounds in spoken words (for example replace the 'm' in mat with 'c' to form a new word cat)

ACELA1458 say words with the same rime as a given word; recognise sound-letter matches including common vowel and consonant digraphs and consonant blends

Expressing and developing ideas

ACELA1438 build word families using onset and rime

ACELA1758 know that spoken words are written down by listening to the sounds heard in the word and then writing letters to represent those sounds

ACELA1778 learn an increasing number of high frequency sight words recognised in shared texts and in texts being read independently

Interpreting, analysing and evaluating

ACELY1649 navigate a text correctly, starting at the right place and reading in the right direction, returning to the next line as needed, matching one spoken word to one written word

ACELY1659 combine knowledge of context, meaning, grammar and phonics to decode text

Word families

tie, pie, lie, kite, bite, white, site, mite, quite, write, invite, ripe, pipe, stripe, hive, five, fire, time, lime, tile, mile, smile, pile, file, while, side, wide, slide, ride, hide, tide, bride, nine, line, pine, dine, fine, mine, shine, spine, vine, twine, shrine, bike, hike, spike

Extra assistance

Creating a word family using the *i-e* split digraph is a big task. Divide the class into small groups and give them a piece of paper and a specific *i-e* rime, eg *ine, ile, ite, ide, ike* and so on. Ask each group to run through the consonants as onset letters and to write down any real words they can make with their *i-e* rime. Put the papers together to make one big *i-e* word family list.

Classroom activities

Bingo!

Give students a laminated board with ten squares on it. Ask them to write a word in each square from a list of *i-e* words (use whiteboard markers). Say words from the list. Students put a cross on that word on their board. First one to ten calls out 'bingo' and wins!

Reading Eggs Lesson sequence	TEACH Content and skills	PRACTISE Children will:	APPLY
Hear: *Animated Lesson*	Review the sound *i-e* with a variety of consonants.	identify the letters that make the *ie* sound. Make *i-e* words. Match *i-e* rimes.	**Worksheet 1** Word families
Write: *Look, Listen and Spell, Word Ladder*	Identify sounds in a word and write the word.	sound out a word and select letters to spell it correctly.	**Worksheet 2** Read and write
Find: *Bowling, 1, 2, 3, 4*	Identify the rime in the word. Identify the order of a sequence of events.	match a word to its rime. Put pictures in order to show a sequence.	**Worksheet 3** Vocabulary
Vocabulary: *Opposite Pairs, Rhyme Time*	Build vocabulary skills: Identify words whose meanings are opposites. Identify rhyming words.	select pairs of cards which are opposites. Find images of rhyming words.	**Worksheet 4** Check
Read: *Bubble Popper, Book*	Read sentences using basic vocabulary. Read aloud book.	read and follow instructions. Listen, follow the reading and read along.	**Reading Eggs book** Word families for ie, ide, ike, ite, ile, ine

Classroom activities

Run to it!

This is best done in a large room with furniture pushed out of the way, or on the playground. Label 4 corners or areas with signs saying *ine, ile, ipe* and *ide.* The students stand in the middle and when the teacher calls out a word containing one of these sounds, they must run to the matching corner.

Related Reading Eggs Activities, Interactives, Songs and Books

Driving Tests

Test 11

Letters and sounds: mite, kite, vine, fine, side, hide, rice, nice, dive, hive

Spelling Bank

Reading Eggs Puzzle Park

Do You Know?

What is it?

More than One

Opposites

Reading Eggs Posters

Reading Eggs Library Books

My Program Books

Teacher Toolkit

- Spelling Activities
- Grammar Lessons
- Comprehension Lessons
- Targeting Comprehension Interactively
- Targeting Text Interactively

Reading Eggs Apps

Eggy Sight words

Eggy Snap

Eggy Phonics 2

Eggy Vocab

Critter Card

Ride the kite bike

i-e

Lesson 87 • Worksheet 1

Name

Word families

1 Join each word to a picture.

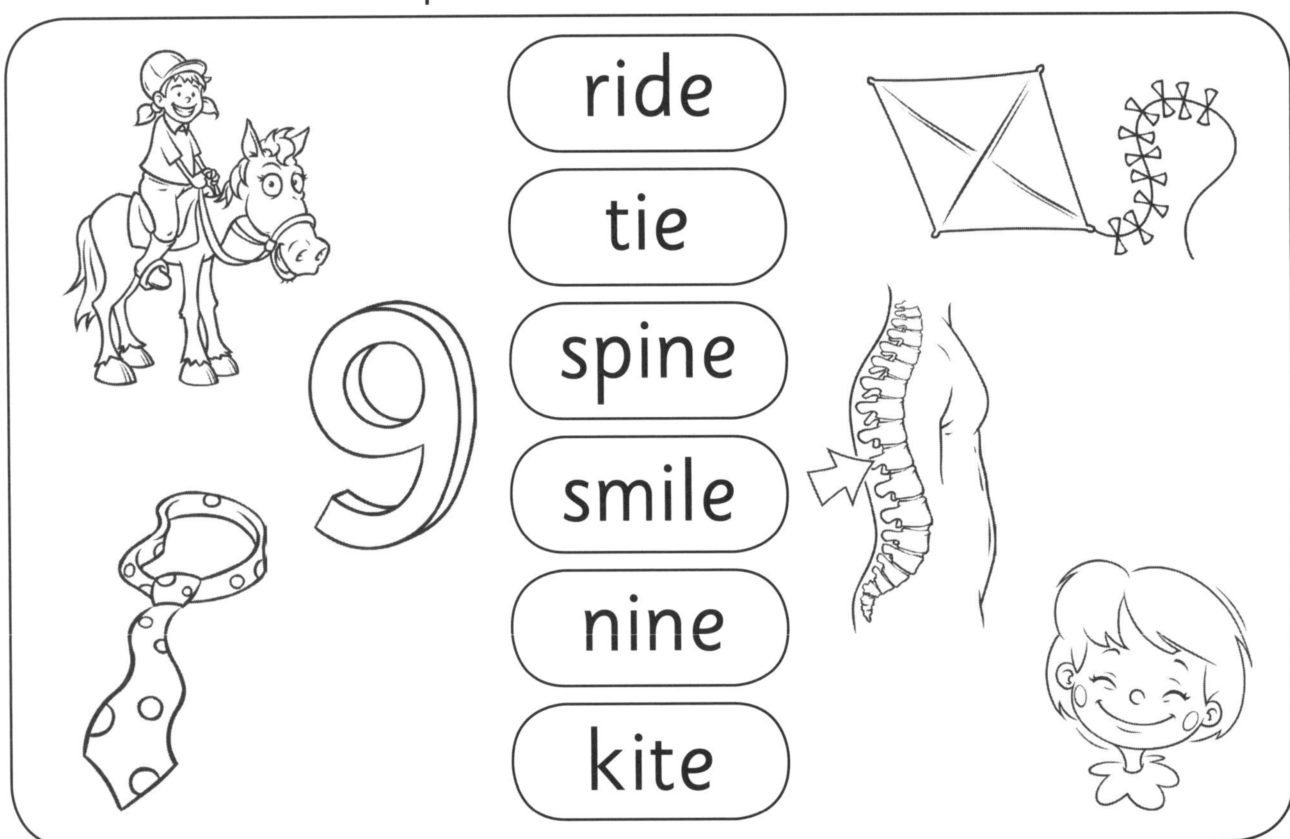

2 Use the word wheels to make words.

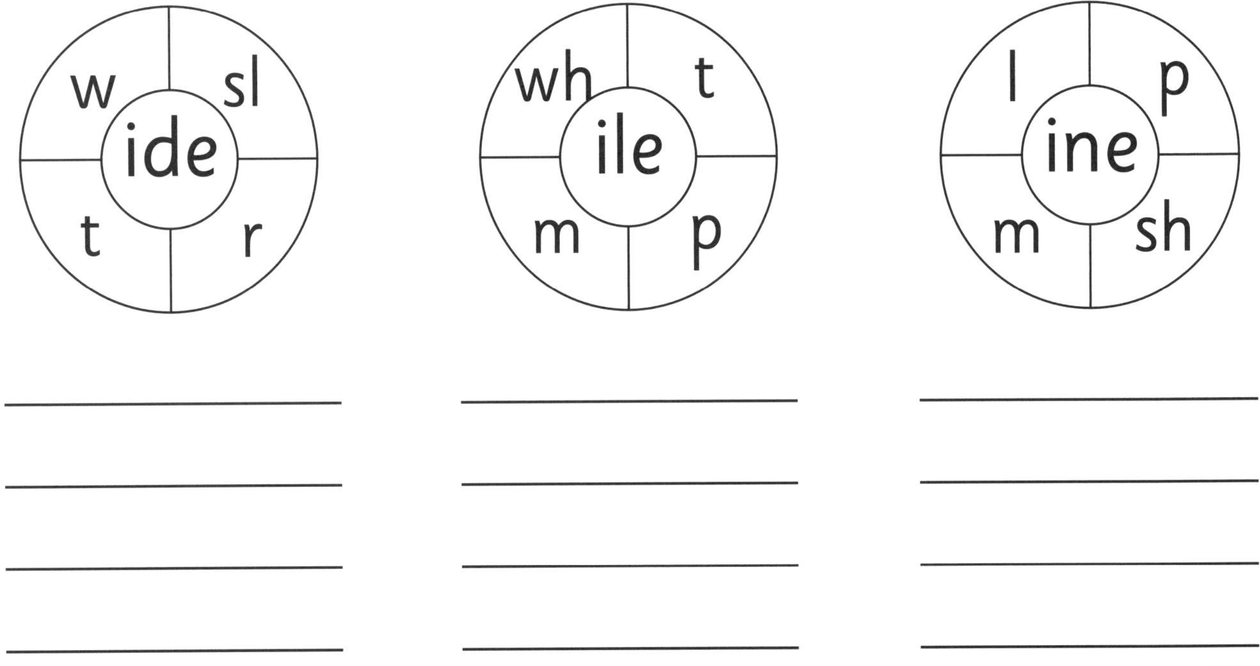

Name

Read and write

i-e

Lesson 87 • Worksheet 2

1 Complete the sentences.

Smile ride bite

Let's go for a __________ in Jet set.

Have a __________ of my apple.

Say hello to __________ the crocodile.

2 Read and draw.

nine striped kites	five white smiles

Vocabulary

Name

Lesson 87 • Worksheet 3

1 Match the opposites.

2 Use the opposites to complete the sentences.

black cold girl hot boy white

The zebra has ______________ and ______________ stripes.

The ______________ is taller than the ______________.

Ice is ______________ and fire is ______________.

Name

Check

i-e

Lesson 87 • Worksheet 4

1 Circle the word that rhymes with the picture.

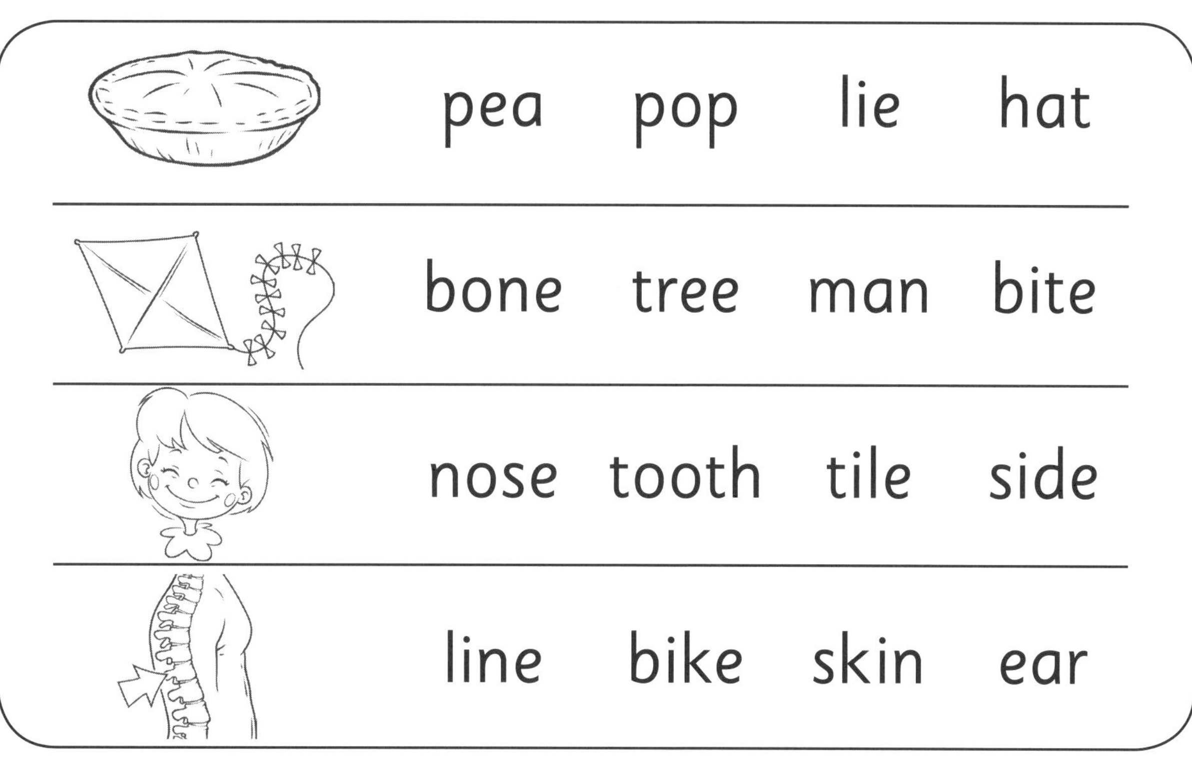

	pea	pop	lie	hat
	bone	tree	man	bite
	nose	tooth	tile	side
	line	bike	skin	ear

2 Colour the beginning sound.

s sh z | d p t | n m i

3 Write a sentence using the words **ride** and **bike**.

Lesson 88 the sound **ch**

Learning objectives

Children will:

- identify the sound ch.
- read and write ch words.

Australian Curriculum Content Descriptions

Sound and letter knowledge

ACELA1439 identify and manipulate sounds (phonemes) in spoken words

ACELA1458 say words with the same rime as a given word; recognise sound-letter matches including common vowel and consonant digraphs and consonant blends

Expressing and developing ideas

ACELA1435 learn that word order in sentences is important for meaning

ACELA1438 build word families using onset and rime

ACELA1455 build word families from common morphemes (for example play, plays, playing, played, playground); use morphemes to read words (for example by recognising the 'stem' in words such as walk/ed)

ACELA1758 know that spoken words are written down by listening to the sounds heard in the word and then writing letters to represent those sounds

ACELA1778 learn an increasing number of high frequency sight words recognised in shared texts and in texts being read independently

Interpreting, analysing and evaluating

ACELY1649 navigate a text correctly, starting at the right place and reading in the right direction, returning to the next line as needed, matching one spoken word to one written word

ACELY1659 combine knowledge of context, meaning, grammar and phonics to decode text

Text Structure and Organisation

ACELA1432 understand that punctuation is a feature of written text different from letters; recognise how capital letters are used for names, and that capital letters and full stops signal the beginning and end of sentences

Sight words

says, ask, what

Word families

cheer, chain, chase, cheek, child, chew, chips, chest, chin, chick, cheese, chat, cheeky, cheeping, chimp, choc, chomp

Extra assistance

The /ch/ sound can be difficult to pronounce, especially for students from some Asian language backgrounds. It is often confused with /sh/ or /j/. To pronounce /ch/ correctly the lips are pursed and teeth slightly apart as for /sh/. It is an unvoiced sound – the vocal cords are not used. Instead of the blow of air as in /sh/, the tongue lifts to block airflow and then drops so the air comes out as a burst of sound.

Classroom activities

Flashcard Snap

Have at least two sets of flashcards for the *ch* words. Shuffle and deal between two players. Keep cards face down. Players take turns to put a card from their pile onto a central pile, saying the word as they turn it over. If the two cards on top are the same, the players shout SNAP! The first to do so takes the central pile. Play continues until one player runs out of cards.

Reading Eggs Lesson sequence	**TEACH Content and skills**	**PRACTISE Children will:**	**APPLY**
Hear: *Animated Lesson*	Introduce the sound *ch*.	identify the sound *ch* in a group. Make *ch* words.	**Worksheet 1** Word families
Write: *Write the Banner*	Recognise correct word order for a sentence.	choose the correct words to make a sentence.	**Worksheet 2** Read and write
Find: *Shooting Stars, Squirter, Buzzy's Word Machine*	Recognise a given word. Identify word endings.	find the given word in a group. Match the word to its ending.	**Worksheet 3** Vocabulary
Vocabulary: *Today's Topic Words, Fishing Boats*	Build vocabulary skills: Recognise key vocabulary.	match pictures to words.	**Worksheet 4** Check
Read: *Book Ends, Book*	Read sentences using basic vocabulary. Read aloud book.	choose a word to finish the sentence. Listen, follow the reading and read along.	**Reading Eggs Story book** Cheeping chicks

Classroom activities

Which Hat?

Place two hats on the floor with the labels *sh* and *ch*. Discuss the sounds. Have a pile of objects or pictures of objects that start with *sh* and *ch*. Each student chooses one object or picture and works out which hat it must go in. Discuss their choice with the class.

Related Reading Eggs Activities, Interactives, Songs and Books

Driving Tests

Test 9

Letters and sounds: chest, chips, chicken, ch

Spelling Bank

Reading Eggs Puzzle Park

Finish the Alien

Do it

What is it?

More than One

Reading Eggs Posters

Reading Eggs Library Books

My Program Books

Teacher Toolkit

- Spelling Activities
- Grammar Lessons
- Comprehension Lessons
- Targeting Comprehension Interactively
- Targeting Text Interactively

Reading Eggs Apps

Eggy Sight words

Eggy Snap

Eggy Phonics 3

Eggy Vocab

Critter Card

Charlie chimp

ch

Name

Word families

Lesson 88 · Worksheet 1

1 Put the word endings through the word machine.
What words can you make?

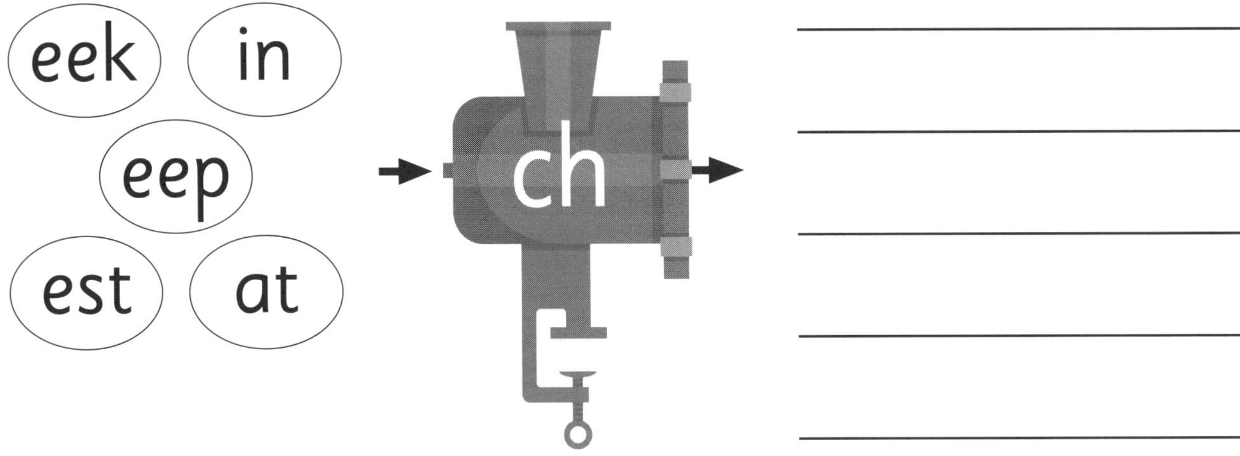

2 Match the words to a picture.

Name

ch

Read and write

Lesson 88 • Worksheet 2

1 Read and draw.

a child with chips	a chimp eating cheese

2 Write a sentence using each word.

chin ______________________________

____

chat ______________________________

____

chomp ______________________________

____

ch

Lesson 88 • Worksheet 3

Name

Vocabulary

Finish the sentences.

cheese chomp chat chin

I can see some

________________________________.

The moon has a big

________________________________.

The horse likes to

________________________________.

They like to

________________________________.

Name

Check

ch

Lesson 88 • Worksheet 4

1 Find the words. Colour the **ch** words green and the **sh** words yellow.

s	h	e	d	c	h	e	e	p	x
z	c	h	i	p	s	h	e	e	p
s	h	o	e	w	c	h	a	i	n
c	h	e	e	k	s	h	i	n	e
w	s	h	o	p	c	h	o	p	u

2 Colour the correct word. Cross out the wrong word.

We buy shoes at the chop / shop .

Cheese is good to chew / shoe .

Chicks go sheep / cheep , cheep / sheep , sheep / cheep .

Lesson 89 the sound **th**

Learning objectives

Children will:

- identify the sound th.
- read and write th words.

Australian Curriculum Content Descriptions

Sound and letter knowledge

ACELA1439 identify and manipulate sounds (phonemes) in spoken words

ACELA1458 say words with the same rime as a given word; recognise sound-letter matches including common vowel and consonant digraphs and consonant blends

Expressing and developing ideas

ACELA1435 learn that word order in sentences is important for meaning

ACELA1438 build word families using onset and rime

ACELA1455 use morphemes to read words (for example by recognising the 'stem' in words such as walk/ed)

ACELA1758 know that spoken words are written down by listening to the sounds heard in the word and then writing letters to represent those sounds

ACELA1778 learn an increasing number of high frequency sight words recognised in shared texts and in texts being read independently

Interpreting, analysing and evaluating

ACELY1649 navigate a text correctly, starting at the right place and reading in the right direction, returning to the next line as needed, matching one spoken word to one written word

ACELY1659 combine knowledge of context, meaning, grammar and phonics to decode text

Text Structure and Organisation

ACELA1432 understand that punctuation is a feature of written text different from letters; recognise how capital letters are used for names, and that capital letters and full stops signal the beginning and end of sentences

Word families

thin, that, thud, thick, thorn, think, thumb, this, there, then

Vocabulary words

kitchen, chocolate, supermarket, sandwich, fridge, roast beef, cupboard, critter, stayed, home, none, two, empty

Extra assistance

Students from some Asian language backgrounds will struggle with the /th/ sound as there is no equivalent in their language. Give them practise in identifying /th/ aurally and in pronouncing it correctly. Use games that rely on correct pronunciation and careful listening such as Bingo with consonants and consonant digraphs, and Go Fish with word family cards for /th/ words.

Classroom activities

Buried Sounds

Collect nine plastic bottle caps and use a permanent marker to write digraphs on top: *sh* x3, *ch* x3, *th* x3. Bury the lids in a container full of rice.

Ask students to search for a top one by one. Then they use magnetic letters to make a word using that digraph. Discuss the word they made.

Reading Eggs Lesson sequence	TEACH Content and skills	PRACTISE Children will:	APPLY
Hear: *Animated Lesson*	Introduce the sound *th* through the song *Throwing makes Charlie thirsty*.	identify the sound *th* in a group. Make *th* words.	**Worksheet 1** Word families
Write: *Bird Words*	Recognise correct word order for a sentence.	choose the correct words to make a sentence.	**Worksheet 2** Read and write
Find: *Bowling, Climb the Ladder, Shooting Stars*	Identify the consonant digraph in the word. Recognise a given word.	match a word to its consonant digraph – *ch, sh, th*. Find the given word in a group.	**Worksheet 3** Vocabulary
Vocabulary: *Today's Topic Words, Words per Minute*	Build vocabulary skills: Recognise key vocabulary.	match pictures to words.	**Worksheet 4** Check
Read: *Book Ends, Book*	Read sentences using basic vocabulary. Read aloud book.	choose a word to finish the sentence. Listen, follow the reading and read along.	**Reading Eggs Story book** This little critter

Lesson 89

Classroom activities

Word Pairs

Give half the class a digraph *sh*, *ch* or *th* on a card. Give the other half of the class a rime – *op, ip, ick, eek, eep, ink, ing*. Ask students to find a partner to make a word and sit together. Ask each digraph person to write their word on the board. Have the pairs swap cards and play again – they must make a different word this time!

Related Reading Eggs Activities, Interactives, Songs and Books

Spelling Bank

Elephants
Lesson 35
Focus sound words: them, thin, thud
Challenge: thunder

Driving Tests

Reading Eggs Puzzle Park

Vegetables
Do You Know?
What is it?
More than One

Music Café

Throwing makes Charlie thirsty

Reading Eggs Library Books

My Program Books

Reading Eggs Posters

Teacher Toolkit

- Spelling Activities
- Grammar Lessons
- Comprehension Lessons
- Targeting Comprehension Interactively
- Targeting Text Interactively

Reading Eggs Apps

Eggy Sight words

Eggy Snap

Eggy Phonics 3

Eggy Vocab

Critter Card

Slip and slide

th

Lesson 89 • Worksheet 1

Name

Word families

1 Match the words to a picture.

2 Write the words.

chicken cherries chips cheese ship shell

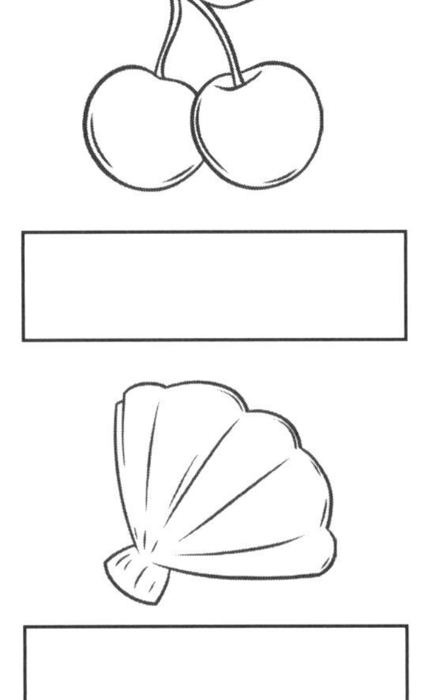

Name

Read and write

Lesson 89 · Worksheet 2

1 Match the sentences to their pictures.

This little critter went to the supermarket.

She got a box of cherries.

He got a box of chocolates.

2 Choose the correct word for each sentence.

stayed	none	empty

This critter __________ home.

This fridge was __________.

This little critter had __________.

Vocabulary

Name

Lesson 89 • Worksheet 3

1 Fill the cupboard. Write the things you can eat on the shelves.

fridge
apple
cheese
hats
chicken
chips
socks
cherries
books
sandwich
peach
chocolate
home
roast beef

2 Write a shopping list for yourself.

Name

Check

Lesson 89 • Worksheet 4

1 Match the words that go together.

none	peach
apple	fridge
shop	empty
cupboard	supermarket

2 Choose the correct word.

Then / That is a good shop.

Then / There is that cheeky chimp.

3 Colour the beginning sound.

sh ch th

sh ch th

sh ch th

Lesson 90 Review

Learning objectives

Children will:

- review the sounds ie, sh, ch and th.
- read and write ch words.

Australian Curriculum Content Descriptions

Sound and letter knowledge

ACELA1439 identify and manipulate sounds (phonemes) in spoken words

ACELA1458 say words with the same rime as a given word; recognise sound-letter matches including common vowel and consonant digraphs and consonant blends

Expressing and developing ideas

ACELA1435 learn that word order in sentences is important for meaning

ACELA1455 build word families from common morphemes (for example play, plays, playing, played, playground); use morphemes to read words (for example by recognising the 'stem' in words such as walk/ed)

ACELA1758 know that spoken words are written down by listening to the sounds heard in the word and then writing letters to represent those sounds

ACELA1778 learn an increasing number of high frequency sight words recognised in shared texts and in texts being read independently

Interpreting, analysing and evaluating

ACELY1649 navigate a text correctly, starting at the right place and reading in the right direction, returning to the next line as needed, matching one spoken word to one written word

ACELY1659 combine knowledge of context, meaning, grammar and phonics to decode text

Text Structure and Organisation

ACELA1432 understand that punctuation is a feature of written text different from letters; recognise how capital letters are used for names, and that capital letters and full stops signal the beginning and end of sentences

Sight words

together, made, these

Word families

chillies, chicken, chocolate, chips, cherries, cheese, chew, chomp, chimp, chilli, cheeky, Charlie,

Vocabulary words

mixed

Extra assistance

To encourage students to think of the consonant digraphs *ch, sh* and *th* as a single unit, make words using these sounds added to the short vowel rimes they have previously learnt. Have them make funny creatures using cut out animal heads with the digraphs on them and animal bodies with rimes on them. Give students freedom to try matching them all up and see which ones make real words.

Classroom activities

Mind the Gap!

Write this sentence on the board: I like chomping on ____. Read the sentence together and brainstorm a list of possible answers.

Students should then copy the sentence: I like chewing on ____. into their book and finish it with their choice of word and matching illustration.

Reading Eggs Lesson sequence	TEACH Content and skills	PRACTISE Children will:	APPLY
Hear: *Animated Lesson*	Review word families, vocabulary and sight words.	identify words learnt in previous lessons.	**Worksheet 1** Word families
Write: *Pick Up Bricks, Bird Words*	Recognise correct word order for a sentence.	choose the correct words to make a sentence.	**Worksheet 2** Read and write
Find: *Frog Logs, Shooting Stars, Buzzy's Word Machine*	Recognise a given word. Identify word endings.	find the given word in a group. Match the word to its ending.	**Worksheet 3** Vocabulary
Vocabulary: *Today's Topic Words, Power Words*	Build vocabulary skills: Recognise key vocabulary.	match pictures to words.	**Worksheet 4** Check
Read: *Book*	Read aloud book.	listen, follow the reading and read along.	**Reading Eggs Story book** Charlie likes cherries

Classroom activities

Say it Right!

Have a set of pictures or a bag of items using the digraphs *sh, ch, th*. Hold up a picture or item and say the word incorrectly, using the wrong digraph, eg ship for chip. Students need to call out the right word.

Related Reading Eggs Activities, Interactives, Songs and Books

Driving Tests

Test 13

Sight words: five

Letters and sounds: dash, flash, pride, bride, while, sheep, bike, like, spine, shine thumb

Content words: dishwasher, knife

Reading Eggs Puzzle Park

Vegetables

Do You Know?

What is it?

More than One

Spelling Bank

Reading Eggs Posters

Reading Eggs Library Books

My Program Books

Teacher Toolkit

- Spelling Activities
- Grammar Lessons
- Comprehension Lessons
- Targeting Comprehension Interactively
- Targeting Text Interactively

Reading Eggs Apps

Eggy Sight words

Eggy Snap

Eggy Phonics 2 and 3

Eggy Vocab

Critter Card

Thingamabob

Review

Lesson 90 • Worksheet 1

Name

Word families

1 Use the word wheels to make words.

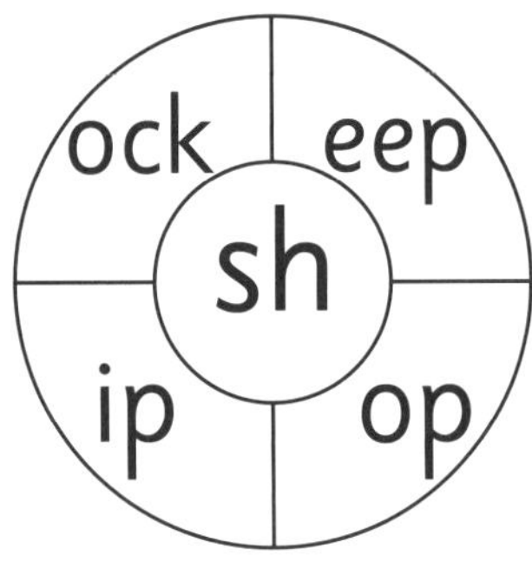

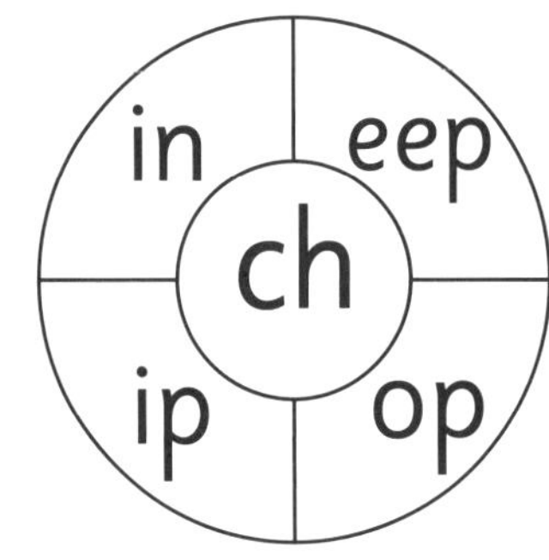

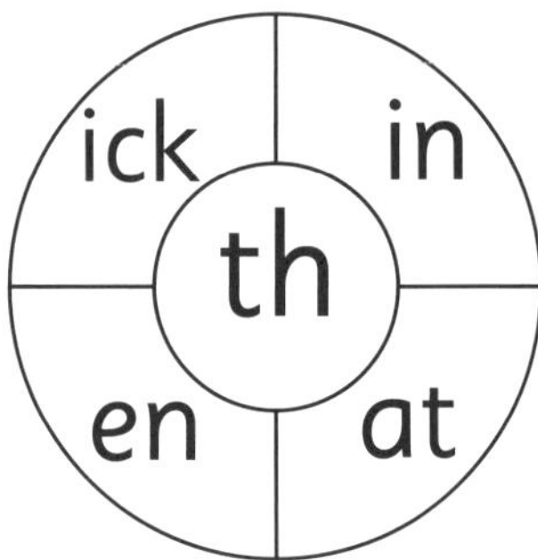

2 Write three more words for each family.

sh________ ch________ th________

sh________ ch________ th________

sh________ ch________ th________

3 Can you think of any words that end in **sh**, **ch** or **th**?

Name

Read and write

Review

Lesson 90 • Worksheet 2

1 Finish the sentences.

cherries chocolate chicken chips

Charlie likes chewing on

________________ .

Charlie likes chomping on

________________ .

Charlie likes chewing on

________________ .

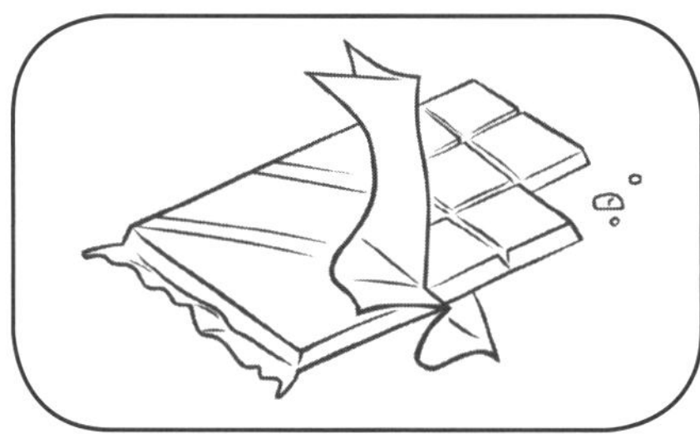

Charlie likes chomping on

________________ .

2 Write the last sentence.

____

____

Review

Lesson 90 · Worksheet 3

Name

Vocabulary

1 Trace and copy.

together

mixed

2 Use the correct word from above to finish the sentences.

Charlie put the cherries and the chocolate ______________.

He ______________ them up.

3 Match the describing word to its item and draw a picture of them.

yuck	chimp
yum	chillies
cheeky	chocolate

Name

Check

Review

Lesson 90 • Worksheet 4

1 Add the correct ending – **ing**, **ed** or **s**.

The chicks are cheep________.

Charlie chew________ the cherries.

He likes chip________.

2 Circle the word that is wrong and write it out correctly.

Charlie is a sheeky chimp. ____________

He likes chomped on chips. ____________

He likes to rid his bike. ____________

Charlie has two cherry. ____________

3 Crack the code!

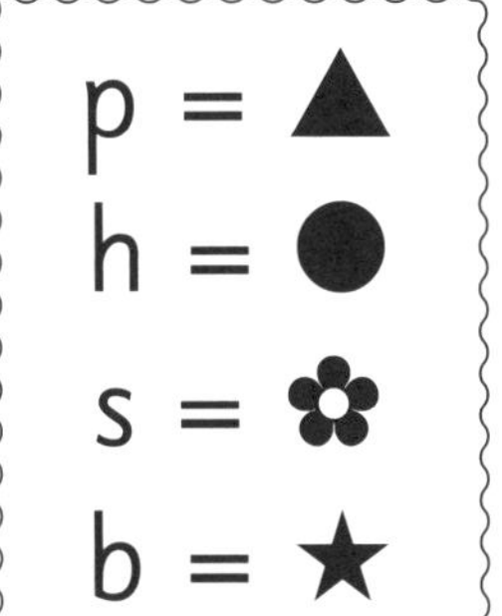

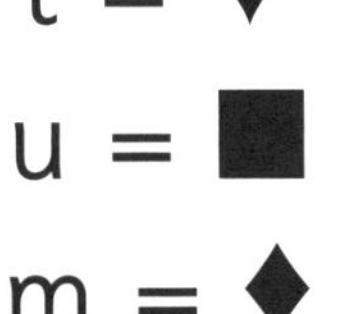

p = ▲
h = ●
s = ✿
b = ★
t = ♥
u = ■
m = ♦

♥●■♦★✿ ■▲!

____

Reading Eggs Posters

In meeting the demands of the Australian Curriculum we have created a poster series as a teaching tool. These full colour, engaging posters can be used on Interactive Whiteboards and tablets as well as printed for classroom use. The series covers the broad scope of curriculum outcomes including language, literature and literacy.

Here is a sample from the series that addresses the construction of proper sentences.

Purpose

To provide a resource for encouraging emerging writers to use proper sentence construction techniques. The posters cover basic parts of speech – nouns, verbs, adjectives, pronouns and the singular and plural forms of words. They also include explanations of various forms of punctuation – capital letters, full stops, question marks and exclamation marks. Teachers can use the overviews of sentence and question structures to bring these aspects of writing together into a cohesive format.

Australian Curriculum Content Descriptions

Text structure and organisation

Understand that punctuation is a feature of written text different from letters; recognise how capital letters are used for names, and that capital letters and full stops signal the beginning and end of sentences (**ACELA1432**)

Expressing and developing ideas

Recognise that sentences are key units for expressing ideas (**ACELA1435**)

Recognise that texts are made up of words and groups of words that make meaning (**ACELA1434**)

Teaching notes

- Use the posters' examples of questions, statements and exclamations to help learners identify the key differences between them, and learn when to use each type of punctuation.
- Discuss usage of capital letters. Give students sentences with no capital letters and ask them to decide which words should have capitals. Discuss their choices as a class and ask students which task the capital letter is fulfilling – sentence beginning, proper noun or the word I.
- The noun, verb and adjective posters come with a companion poster which has an illustration using these words. Ask small groups of students to write as many of that type of word as they can based on the companion poster.
- Annotate text samples together as a class. Choose simple texts such as nursery rhymes and highlight the parts of speech and punctuation used. Advanced students could be asked to repeat this activity in pairs or individually.
- Print the Reading and Spelling Strategies posters in A3 format to put up on the wall. Use them as a reminder before students begin writing or reading activities. Refer students to the strategies during writing and reading activities to build independence.
- Cut the high frequency words lists into 24 smaller lists and play word detectives. Give each student a list and a book and ask them to find as many of the words as they can. When students are writing independently direct them to these two posters to help them spell common words.

The posters

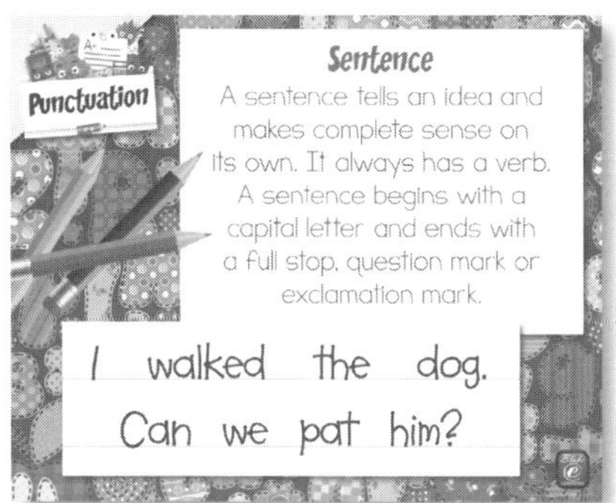

Sentences

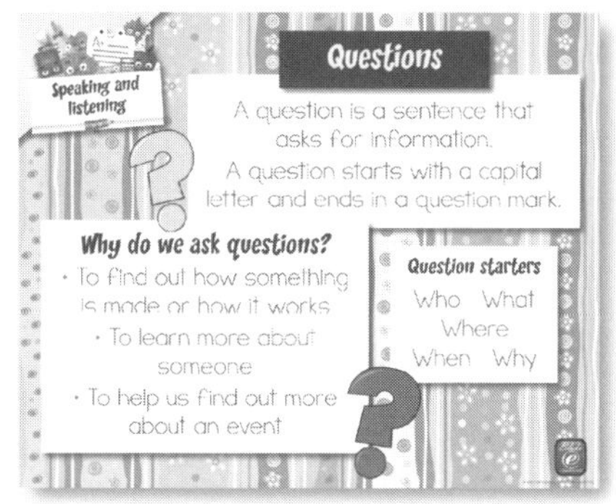

Questions

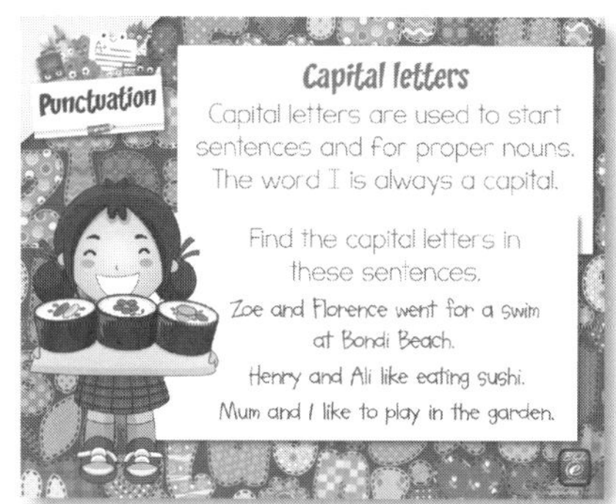

Capital Letters

Verbs

Pronouns

Singular and Plural

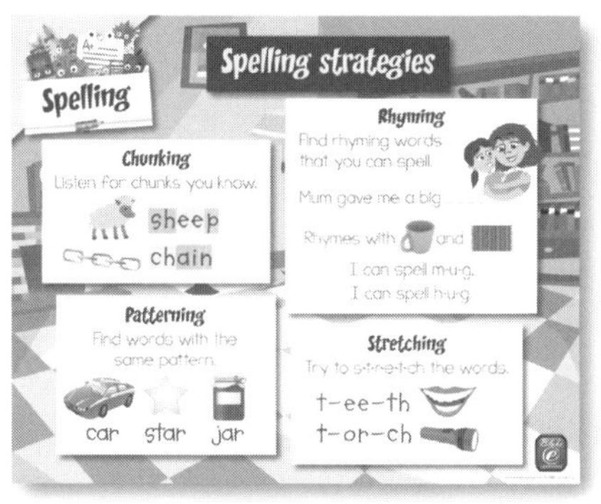

Spelling Strategies

Reading Strategies

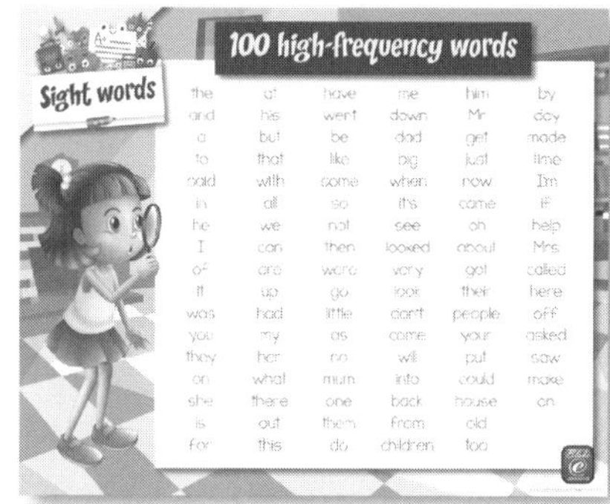

High Frequency Words

Skills Checklist Lessons 61-90

Name

Lesson	Skills	Check
61	Writes and recognises sight words – me, be, look. Completes and comprehends sentences. Identifies theme words – action verbs. Writes their own sentences.	
62	Recognises and writes -ut and -up words. Identifies beginning sounds – m, c, s, t. Reads colour words – blue, red, green. Reads number words – six, ten, three.	
63	Recognises and writes -ug and -un words. Completes and comprehends sentences. Identifies theme words – action verbs. Recognises and writes -ip words.	
64	Writes and uses the sight words – to, at, in, on. Recognises sight words. Completes sentences. Reads and comprehends short u words.	
65	Recognises and writes -uck words. Identifies rhyming words. Writes words in correct order to make sentences. Matches onset and rime to make short u words.	
66	Writes and uses the sight words – there, that, this. Writes words in correct order to make sentences. Identifies theme words – nature. Uses describing words – colours, big, little, tall.	
67	Writes and uses theme words – facial features. Uses words for amounts – one, two, ten, lots. Recognises when to use have or has. Writes colour words.	
68	Reads and comprehends sentences. Recognises number, colour and body part words. Writes their own sentences. Completes sentences.	
69	Writes and recognises sight words – do. Completes and comprehends sentences. Recognises and uses action verbs. Identifies when to use can or cannot.	
70	Reviews short u words. Completes sentences and writes their own. Uses sight words correctly. Identifies number, colour and action words.	
71	Recognises when to use play/plays, come/comes. Completes and comprehends sentences. Identifies theme words – party. Identifies the number of sounds in words.	
72	Writes -ed and -eg words. Writes words in correct order to make sentences. Adds -ing to verbs and uses them in sentences. Recognises -ing, -ed and -eg words.	
73	Writes -et words. Identifies rhyming words and the days of the week. Comprehends sentences and writes their own. Recognises short e words.	
74	Writes -et and -eg words. Completes sentences. Recognises theme words – pets. Identifies end sounds.	
75	Writes and reads -en words. Adds -ing to verbs and uses them in sentences. Writes and uses the sight words – where, when, up, down. Recognises vowels in words.	

Name

Skills Checklist Lessons 61-90

Lesson	Skills	Check
76	Writes and recognises -en and -eg words. Writes words in correct order to make sentences. Reads and comprehends sentences. Recognises colour words.	
77	Completes sentences. Recognises theme words – animals and their homes. Writes and uses the sight words – who, lives, here. Uses verbs correctly.	
78	Uses sight words correctly – what, when, who, where. Completes sentences. Identifies theme words – dragon parts and colours. Recognises theme words – animals.	
79	Writes and uses sight words – what, when, who, where. Writes -ell words. Recognises theme words – animals and numbers. Comprehends sentences.	
80	Recognises and writes short e words. Completes sentences. Uses theme words – party. Recognises number and colour words.	
81	Matches onset and rime to make short vowel words. Recognises and uses sight words – with, what, have. Completes sentences. Recognises and writes theme words – body parts and senses.	
82	Recognises and writes -ie words. Writes words in correct order to make sentences. Completes and comprehends sentences. Recognises theme words – pie shop and describing words.	
83	Recognises and writes -ie and -i-e words. Comprehends sentences and writes their own. Recognises theme words – family.	
84	Writes -ie, -ike and -ine words. Identifies vowel sounds. Completes and comprehends sentences. Identifies number of sounds in words.	
85	Recognises and writes sh- words. Comprehends sentences. Writes words in correct order to make sentences. Writes their own sentences.	
86	Recognises and writes sh- words. Identifies theme words – animals and clothing. Completes sentences. Writes words in correct order to make sentences.	
87	Recognises and writes -ie and -i-e words. Completes sentences and writes their own. Identifies opposites and uses them correctly. Recognises rhyming words.	
88	Recognises and writes ch- words. Writes their own sentences. Completes sentences. Identifies ch- and sh- words.	
89	Recognises th- words. Writes ch- and sh- words. Comprehends and completes sentences. Recognises theme words – food.	
90	Writes and recognises sh-, ch- and th- words. Completes sentences and writes their own. Uses sight words correctly – together, mixed. Identifies the correct word endings from -ing, -ed, -s.	

Name

Read the text.

I like the red leaves in the forest.
I like the green water in the lake.
I like the brown branches in the trees.
I like the colours of the sunsets.

Underline the correct answer.

1 What is green?
- the lake water
- the branches
- the sunsets

2 What colour are the leaves?
- green
- brown
- red

3 Where are the branches?
- in the lake
- in the trees
- in the sunsets